50 Feet In 4 Seconds

The True Story of a Leap into
Consciousness and Ultimate Health

by
Sheryl Jai, RMT,
Melchizedek Priestess

MAGIC VALLEY PUBLISHERS

Sale of this book without a front cover may be unauthorized. If this book is without a cover, it may have been reported to the publisher as "unsold or destroyed" and neither the author nor the publisher may have received payment for it.

>Published by Magic Valley Publishers
>Copyright 2007 © by Sheryl Jai
>All Rights Reserved.

Except for use in any review, the reproduction of this work in whole or in part in any form by any electronic, mechanical or other means, now known or hereafter invented, including xerography, photocopying and recording, or in any information storage or retrieval system, is forbidden without the written permission of the publisher, Magic Valley Publishers, 6390 E Willow St, Long Beach CA 90815 U.S.A.

ISBN 0-9785509-2-7

Manufactured in the United States of America
Second Edition

>To contact Sheryl Jai aka Shazna Jai (pronounced Shayna):
>541-482-2301
>sheryljai@gmail.com or shaznaj@earthlink.net
>www.50feetin4seconds.com
>www.sheryljai.byregion.net
>www.thejaiconsciousnessfoundation.org
>www.haveawish.org

Endorsements

"An amazing, powerful and inspiring story about Waking Up."
Gerald G. Jampolsky, M.D. Founder of Center for Attitudinal Healing and author of *"Love is Letting Go of Fear."*

"The story is beautiful and it's written beautifully. It will make a difference to many people."
Carol Adler, Dandelion Press

"I read your book on the way home from Dallas....it is wonderful...inspiring, profound and remarkable. Bless you, bless you."
Rita Reneaux, Relationship Expert and Coach

"We have both finished your book. I was deeply touched. I came to tears of joy many times while reading your story. It confirmed my belief that we are meant to be healthy, wealthy and happy, and it is our unexamined beliefs that hold us back. You demonstrated the ability to transcend the drama of the experience and to look beyond into the blessing. It is a very powerful wonderful book. I feel grateful to have you share this story with me."
Will & Cate McClard

"When I read Sheryl Jai's extraordinary account of her fall and her healing I felt I was there with her. She beautifully describes each moment, each feeling, each insight. I felt I was with this courageous woman as she opened herself to another way of being. Through her eyes, I saw other possibilities, other meanings to life experiences."
Anita Tamboli, Transformational Life Coach

Endsorsements

"Sheryl Jai's healing journey is an inspiration. Her story shows us how to partner with our body as it heals, and the miracles that are possible when we do. This book has transformed my relationship to pain and helped me remember there is always a gift in adversity."

Nancy Grace, Muse

"The story took me through your amazing healing and transformation. As the author of this amazing story that you have lived, you definitely have something to share with all of us as about how we can move through pain and challenge to the other side. Thank you for sharing your story...may it assist and serve many on this planet."

Virginia 'Joy' Smith, Author *"The Dolphin Lady"*

"I know Sheryl as a friend, teacher, spiritual counselor, and now as an excellent storyteller. The truth of her experience drifts up from the pages as you read them, and you find yourself being there as a witness to miracles. Somehow, you know that this can be everyone's truth of experience, with Sheryl as your able guide. Let your Self be touched by her story, with a knowingness that it could be your story, as well."

Peggy Phillips, Treasury Manager for CCA Global Partners, Inc.

". . . This story is so inspiring . . . it's not more, more, more of the same . . . the energy within the text has a transmission in it . . . your experience is completely embodied . . ."

Nancy Clemens, Author *"Dolphin Divination Cards"* and *"A Guide to the Dolphin Divination Cards"*

"A deeply moving testimonial to each person's ability to physically heal their own body. Sheryl's personal triumph forms the path for each of us to follow as we heal our bodies and minds and reconnect to spirit."
Dr. Talia Miller, Holistic Wellness Recovery Coach

"Sheryl's story has been an inspiration for me to take a deeper look at the messages my body gives me. Through Sheryl, I have learned that my body is telling me where I am holding emotions that need to be released, and to allow Spirit to flow in its wonderful, gentle ways. Sheryl's depth of overcoming and clarity has been a guidepost for me to move easier along my spiritual path to fully be the oneness of Spirit."
Patricia Haller, Reiki Master, Licensed Unity Teacher

"I was reading your book again today and I just want to tell you how much it touches me. I feel such grace when I'm reading it! It brought me to tears! What an amazing woman and what an amazing book. I hope that it touches and changes sooooo many peoples' lives!"
Joette Treiber, Retired Psychologist

"I finished your book. It was great to see how you healed your body. I loved all the soul searching concepts. Gives me much hope that we can all heal. I believe we can heal ourselves. Some of us just need a nudge in the right direction. Thank you so much for journaling your experiences, for the rest of us to follow."
Linda Bazan, Entrepreneur

Endorsements

"Thank you for writing your book. Thank you for your love. Congratulations on following your heart and your bliss all these years. Many blessings to you."
    Suzanne McMillan-McTavish, Sedona Author and Sedona Vortex Tour/Spiritual Guide

"What an amazing story! This is a new beginning for me. I will do this meditation faithfully every day. And I will get the help I need. Thank you so much for writing this book! It must have been a tremendous task to describe your inner experiences in such a way that uninitiated people can appreciate them. But it all sounds truthful, that's very important."
    Magdalene Jaeckel, 83, Homemaker

Table of Contents

Forward by Dr. Timothy Bonatus	9
Introduction	12
Chapter 1: Dreaming of Angels, Hiking and more Angels	16
Chapter 2: The Fall, Awakening, and Rescue	27
Chapter 3: Hospital, Surgery, and Miracle Healing	45
Chapter 4: Home Recovery with Angels	56
Chapter 5: Learning Divine Skills	64
Chapter 6: Sub-conscious to Conscious	75
Chapter 7: Asking for Grace in Final Surgery	93
Chapter 8: Ceremony on the Mountain	98
Chapter 9: Receiving Grace in Final Surgery	102
Chapter 10: Learning to Unlearn	106
Chapter 11: Divine Message	112
Chapter 12: Simple Daily Healing Practices	
Utilizing Universal Principles	117
Discernment Technique	125
Asking Yourself Empowering Questions	130
Conscious Breathing	133
Chakra Toning and Clearing	136
Self-Healing Meditation	139
Postscript	147
Appendix: The New Teacher	151
Acknowledgements	156
Recommended Reading	159
Glossary	160

50 Feet in 4 Seconds

This book is dedicated to God, my children, Kimberly and Tod Kubo, and the children who are our future. May they always know who they are.

And to my family . . . whose hearts have loved and been broken, experienced betrayal and loneliness, lived with distrust and deceit, courage and strength, and have healed each in their own way for the betterment of their lives and the lives of their children.

50 Feet in 4 Seconds

Forward

This is the story of Sheryl Jai's remarkable recovery from multiple injuries sustained in a fall in Sedona, Arizona. While Sheryl's injuries were significant, the process and means of her recovery is worthy of study.

Though the details are contained in this book, in brief, this is Sheryl's orthopaedic history: On April 26, 1997, while hiking with friends, the then 47-year-old fell approximately 50 feet off a cliff in Sedona, Arizona. She was attended by her friends until firefighters and medics rescued her. She was flown by helicopter to the regional trauma center in Flagstaff, Arizona, where I was the Orthopaedic Surgeon on call. Sheryl was remarkably calm for the magnitude of her multiple injuries. She experienced the typical trauma patient evaluation and resuscitation when she arrived in the trauma bay. However, while the trauma team tries to be sensitive about patients' privacy and personal needs, this is an invasive and dehumanizing experience where the primary goal is to quickly diagnose, stabilize, and begin treatment of life-threatening injuries.

In spite of the height of her fall and multiple fractures, Sheryl had no significant internal injuries noted on physical exam or CT scan. Her injuries included an open (compound) fracture of the right proximal ulna (elbow) with bone loss and an open scapula (shoulder blade) fracture. She also had multiple pelvic fractures, fractures of both feet and ankles, and lumbar spine fractures. She was treated with emergent surgery of her open fractures. The elbow was repaired

Forward

surgically with a bone graft, plates and screws. Open fractures are not infrequently returned to the OR for a second "washout." Sheryl's course demonstrated no fever or clinical signs of infection. Therefore, the second debridement (the removal of damaged tissue or foreign objects from a wound) surgery was not undertaken. Her positive attitude and aggressive physical therapy led to an early hospital discharge. Miraculously, she left walking, with platform crutches and a short leg cast on her left leg.

Sheryl was nearly always smiling at her follow-up visits. Her fractures healed in record time. Though sometimes struggling with the pain, physical limitations, and associated enforced lifestyle changes, she remained positive in the face of tremendous daily challenges. She had an amazing energy about her. It was palpable in the exam room.

Sheryl's injuries had the potential for serious infection, lack of proper bone healing, loss of motion, and post-traumatic pain and arthritis. She required a second surgery in October of 1997 to remove the orthopaedic implants from her right elbow. To date, she has not experienced any of the potential sequelae (a pathological condition resulting from a prior disease, injury, or attack) of her injuries. As an Orthopaedic Traumatologist, I treat a lot of patients with multiple injuries. Where I live and practice, the majority of these are a mix of motor vehicle injuries, falls, horseback riding, and skiing injuries. It is fascinating how differently people respond to their injuries. Some see the experience as a challenge and rise to it, others are angry and full of blame; some are independent and want to "do it themselves," while still others rely on friends and family for physical, emotional, and even financial support. Some patients take on a "sick" mindset and others choose to strive for wellness. I see the same injury, in different people, become inconsequential or disabling, depending upon the patient's mind set, not the injury itself.

Sheryl made an amazingly rapid and complete recovery, the details of which she has graciously shared in this book. We can all learn from her experience.

Dr. Timothy Bonatus
Orthopaedic Surgeon

Introduction

Can you imagine what it would be like to be pregnant for eight years? Giving birth to this book took eight very long years. There were many painful "dark nights of the soul" to accept and bring myself from an emotionally unstable person, to someone who appreciates every experience I have had as a learning tool to hold more light and love inside me. This process was very personal and I did not want to write about it, experiencing it was enough. Most times I felt I did not have the words that would accurately express the dimensions that I experienced. This writing is a novice approach to tell a phenomenal story in a simple way. Many times I felt the words I wrote were inadequate to express the magnitude of the experience, it was frustrating. I would stop at these times, use the processes I learned and allow that energy to dissipate, then, begin again in a fresh moment. I challenged myself to be clear, quiet, and peaceful as I wrote so that the energy of God's grace could be imparted from me in its purity. I will explain further below about the energy of this book and how to use it.

My intention in writing this book is to offer you, the reader, a space for opening to your own personal experience of consciousness and healing. It is my suggestion that you utilize the "notes" pages I've added for your convenience to jot down what comes to you as you are reading. Use these pages as a type of journal, writing whatever comes to you: feelings, sensations, or thoughts. In this way, you are paying close attention to your own experience as you read. Feel what is there, see how you are being reminded of something from your past to heal: whatever comes up, make some notes. I have also added a glossary for some terms that I use that you may not be familiar with or that have a dual meaning. This glossary is to empower you to be clear with yourself. Since our minds love to make up stories and meanings about everything in our lives, I was guided to add the glossary to keep the experience congruent, that is, in alignment with the energy of the story itself. I also found the glossary a wonderful place for me to continue to express some of the ways I've used these terms as practices. I hope you enjoy reading it as much as I did writing it.

There are many ways you can read and interpret the information presented besides what I will mention here. One way is to be the observer, one who reads and comprehends some but mostly is unaffected. Another way is to be closely involved so that you begin to experience your own reaction to what you are reading. Another possibility would be to read a bit, integrate the information, make notes, then read further. You also might experience some energy working through you. This is perfect for you to be aware of in each moment you are reading. And . . . there are many other possibilities. Some people have shared with me they could not even stay awake while reading. Saying they had to go to sleep, then when they woke start all over. Some say they have read it more than once to integrate deeper the healing they felt was possible for them. Whatever happens is perfect for you, your

Introduction

consciousness and the changes and healing you are creating in your life.

What I've just explained is what I learned through my own process of writing this book. It never occurred to me to write a book about the process of healing. It came as a result of requests from students, after taking my classes to learn this material. While writing was more of a struggle for me than speaking or teaching, I found that writing became a healing tool as well. There were times when I wasn't sure if I was writing this book, or it was writing me. I kept healing deep core levels of myself, using each principle that I learned. What you have in your hands is my "heart and soul." It is my gift to share with you.

I am ready to release this book from the heart of my womb. To offer you the best of what I can give, trusting that you will get exactly what you are ready for, from this book, and from your life. If reading my story will help just one person, I am happy.

I want to thank you for choosing my book. I would appreciate hearing from you and having you tell me your story and what you have learned—either from my story or your relationship with God and your precious path. (I referenced the name of God throughout this book, as my relationship with God has no gender or religious overtones. Please feel free to substitute your word, which represents that which is bigger than you.)

Mostly, I am happy that you are interested in recognizing who you really are, acknowledging your diving connection, waking up, staying awake, and living in a healthy body! Committing to your precious life path is really a life long commitment, without instant gratification. If you can handle that, you will win! May you receive all you intend,

Sheryl Jai,
November, 2006

Chapter 1

Angels, a Dream, a Hike and more Angels

*Once upon a time there was a little girl,
when she was very small she knew
she knew, what she knew.
One day, someone said, "You don't know what you know,
maybe . . . one day. . . when you're big", so she forgot.
One day when she was big, she knew she remembered
and she said, "I know that I know what I know. . . Now!"*

I awake from a deep sleep, looking around, feeling alert, yet curious. I see that I'm in the hospital. I wonder for a moment, and then remember how I got there. As I'm feeling my body, I'm checking if what I remember is correct. My body is broken. Did I have an accident? Oh my gosh, I fell off a cliff! Pausing, breathing I ask myself "Was it a dream?"

For a moment the memory seems foggy. No, it is real. The scenes flash in my mind, one by one. It *was* real. The shock of seeing my body lying in this bed and knowing I won't be moving is comforted by a strange sense that I am not frightened or in pain. My mind is having a struggle with the reality or non-reality of this experience. Is this really happening to me? What is actually happening? I feel wonderful, yet I'm lying in a hospital bed, broken, but strangely, barely bruised.

50 Feet in 4 Seconds

I remember hiking . . . flying from a cliff to the rocks below . . . being rescued by some very nice people and flown in a helicopter . . . being in an emergency room . . . having surgery. And now I'm here.

Adjusting my eyes and my senses to the room, I realize I'm safe. I smell the essence of lavender. I see many beautiful fresh flowers. I see my ex-husband and some friends, smiling and surrounding me on all sides. I hear loving voices. People are so happy to see my eyes open and a smile appear on my face. I am loved. I feel strangely happy. I am alive . . . but what really happened?

When I awoke to the bright sun coming through my window that Saturday morning, I was reviewing a dream that nagged to be part of my consciousness. I was in an office building up about five stories high. I saw the translucent figures of angels against a clear blue sky of daylight. I turned and asked my co-workers in the office to come and look at what I was seeing. No one came. I thought to myself, "This must be just for me."

There were seven angels standing (floating) in the blue sky, shoulder to shoulder, beaming the most brilliant shimmering light, their faces beautifully content and welcoming. There were five or six others apparently lying in a horizontal position at the feet of the seven standing. As I marveled at each angel looking at me with such intense love, my heart felt they were

Angels, a Dream, a Hike and more Angels

speaking to me. I did not know what they were saying. I just felt something curiously special and wonderful touching me.

As I ate a leisurely breakfast, I glanced outside beyond the glass doors of my living room to the garden that I recently replanted. The garden was calling me to come outside and water. After I finished eating I walked outside and reached for the garden hose. I have a goddess statue gracefully sitting amidst the regal purple iris, native cholla and prickly pear cactus, aloe, and delicate miniature roses. Today as I watered, I playfully make an arc with the water and noticed there was rainbow light, just above the garden.

Was it the water today? Was it the garden today? Why, after years of watering, is it that today I see a rainbow over my garden? I watched the colors of the rainbow brighten and soften, glistening and dancing with the water. The feeling of love for nature is moving through my body, and I am so happy I have scheduled a hike for this perfect day with friends.

My friends and I met precisely at 1 pm. at the trailhead. Karon is a long time friend with a beautifully enthusiastic smile, a tiny yet strong frame, and a delightful southern drawl. We met in our Chiropractor's office about a year before. Most weeks we had an appointment at the same time. At these times we were excited to see each other and enjoyed sitting next to each other gradually getting to know each other planning things to do outside of the doctor's office.

50 Feet in 4 Seconds

At the start of our hike Karon proclaims she is in training for a rigorous hike up one of the largest mountains in red rock country, and she plans to accomplish this in five hours. (I heard that the best hikers in the area take 8 hours!) She is determined and goes after whatever she desires with much enthusiasm and dedication. Through my life coaching work with Karon, we developed a high level of communication and trust between us. We have worked out many of her life concerns together. We decide that after the hike we will stop for some food and talk about insights revealed through this experience. Little did we know that what was to come would alter our lives forever.

Another friend, Bob, joins us on our hike. He is an acquaintance. He hikes regularly and has hiked most of the mountains in the area. His delightful intellect and witty humor are wonderfully welcome to complete our synchronistic trio. He and Karon are meeting today for the first time because they share a love of the land, and me. Spending the afternoon with friends on the land is a unifying as well as humbling experience because of the deeper connection we share. Karon and Bob were to become bonded by the end of this day.

It is a beautiful sunny day, delightfully warm, the spring season approaching. Hiking with friends is common for each of us, and having the weather be so perfect, is a bonus. In talking before we set out on this adventure, we chose unanimously to do this hike in complete silence. None of us had done a silent hike before, especially on what might be considered difficult terrain, but we were game. Our rules included hand

Angels, a Dream, a Hike and more Angels

signaling each other if we needed assistance or anything else, and of course, warnings if there was danger. We agreed to keep our attention on our feet, the land, the beauty of the area, and whatever may be going on in our minds and body's to have a total experience.

The beginning of this hike is an easy fifteen-minute walk on level land. Among the forest and the varied brush there is a sinkhole, a phenomenon of nature where the land cracks wide open to reveal fresh earth. Its opening is about 20 feet across and 25–30 feet down. This happened so long ago that trees of cypress and pine are fully grown down deep inside the sinkhole. It seems the earth split there some thousand years ago and the winds of nature used the seeds of the trees of the flat land above to repair itself.

A few yards ahead we approach the seven pools. They are natural waterfalls. When the snow melts off from the winter season and trickles down the mountainside, it dribbles into each of these ponds carved naturally into the side of the sloping mountain. Many tourists in the area are fond of taking pictures of these two sites, as this trail is also a heavily traveled "jeep-tour" locale. Walking another twenty minutes we come to areas where the boulders are so huge they are like land floors. Many people sunbathe from this spot and take pictures of the mountains that surround this trail of beauty. Beyond this is where the challenge of the hike begins.

We leave the flatland to begin a 30% uphill grade. Although the trails are clearly marked, the paths are narrow. There are small pebbles, shale, and slippery rocks on the mountainside, along the way. The trees are close together, and because the land is steep here, our awareness and full attention keep us steadily focused on the ground. My former husband, Stan, found this pristine spot. We hiked here many times to improve our hiking skills. I also have taken many people on this hike to challenge them and offer them an adventure in nature. Today I feel sure-footed and gleefully intrigued as my sense of myself on the mountain is confident. Karon and Bob seem to be thoroughly enjoying the hike as well. We periodically stop to drink water, and glance at each other's eyes to see if a signal of need or warning was present, or to proceed. We communicate care for each other in subtle and very obvious nuances of body language.

After about thirty minutes of climbing uphill, the mountain becomes more rugged and requires even more mindfulness of our footing on the land. Entering the magnificence of the mountain where rocks from some thirty million years ago have fallen and worn away from wind, snow, and rain, is a mighty adventure. Centuries ago, the Native American Anasazi tribe made their homes here, raised children and hunted for food from these very caves and forests through which we are walking. This is where animals of many breeds roam freely on the land. It is also a mass of forest and trees providing oxygen for thousands of people.

People come to these sites to be in the presence of Godly nature as it is—raw, complete, perfect—and they come to challenge themselves with the terrain. I come for a combination of both. To me a day of physical

Angels, a Dream, a Hike and more Angels

activity and loving the land, plants and animals *is* accomplishment. I feel some of nature's love rubs off on my mundane everyday life, and it makes my world brighter.

The difficulty of the hike does not keep us from being awed by the welcoming appearance of an opening in the mountain. It is hollowed out from cave dwellers and years of wind roaring though its mouth. Climbing up to enter this cave requires strength and agility. Bob, Karon, and I all have different strengths and abilities in our bodies. To make it up the huge first boulder to enter the cave, I use my knees, and then I lift myself with my strong arms. Bob takes a step with his long legs and reaches the next level in one leap. Karon turns and uses her behind and fit legs to bring her body up the four-foot step to accept the cave's invitation of walking on higher ground. We pause to absorb the feelings of accomplishment as we stand quietly, and look at the awesome beauty of Mother Natures' carvings inside the cave . . . how the wind has artfully drawn many layers of iron, magnesium, and zinc into a picture-like form. We agree it looks like a womb to us—if you could see inside one!

Walking further, we come to a precipice, spanned by a twelve-inch wide ledge, with a layered drop off of 35 to 50 feet. This ledge is just wide enough for our feet. It is breathtakingly beautiful, and scary. To enjoy the view, I am both still and calm as I am keenly aware I could fall with the slightest misstep. There is nothing to hold on to but my own self-centered, grounded energy. As we walk this tiny ledged passage, to my right is the mountain's wall—about 70 feet high—and below, a steep drop of 35-50 feet covered with rocks, shale, dirt, cactus, and trees. Some people cross this path on their hands and knees, as it probably is the safest way. The fear level within begins to rise as we inch our way across the ledge. Although it is only about 20 feet long, it is God's way of reminding me that every moment counts here.

When on the other side of this ledge we look into each other's eyes, nonverbally connecting with relief. I see enthusiasm, mixed with fear, and a sort of confidence in my friends, that I also feel. I am happy about their comfort level on the trail, knowing that the upcoming terrain would be more demanding of their strength. The next part of the hike seemed to propel and even inspire movement as graceful as trained athletes over these enormous boulders with large troughs between them. Nothing seems to get in the way of having more energy to accomplish this difficult terrain. In fact, something seems to inspire an attitude in us of empowerment.

We climb several higher peaks, coming to the most difficult one of all. We literally etch our footsteps into the mountain's side, and reach the mesa. With a feeling of exhilaration we take in the magnificence of the mesa. We are clearly seeing at least one hundred miles in each direction. We view the scenery of ages in the past, sensing the history—forest and blue skies—we breathe pure, clean fresh air. These mountains are known to be over three hundred and thirty million years old. It is documented that the ocean has come and gone from

Angels, a Dream, a Hike and more Angels

this area at least three times. Many times people find fossilized seashells on the land as proof, as well as arrowheads, and even artifacts of Native American ruins. It is rich with history, lore, and vibrant energy.

Karon, Bob, and I find a comfortable spot to rest, drink water, and have a snack. Still in silence, our senses seem to heighten, with acute attention paid to the area's energy having a quality of aliveness. We did not know we would have the opportunity to learn about ourselves in a new way today. Being in silence in such a magnificent area, moving the physical body in this way, allows us to have an understanding of what it must be like to be and live like the animals. That sense animals live by—that feeling of instinct, a knowing where to find food, and when to leave an area as the seasons change—protects them from being preyed upon by larger animals, or even allows them to surrender to be preyed upon. Nesting happens by an inner harmony that animals are born with and survive on. I wonder if this instinct could be imbedded within me, and if so, I yearn to know more about it.

Having grown up in the 60's in southern California and also having raised my family there, moving to the small town of Sedona, Arizona, filled with friendly people, mountains, and seasons—was a strange and new environment for me, and I welcomed the change. It allowed a side of me to further expand I hadn't known and my awareness was intensified this day. Today I feel even more aware of my surroundings and realize how most of my life I have made material things so important. Today I was watching and learning . . . something very new.

After about an hour meditating, and eating a snack on the mesa, we signal to each other we are ready for the climb down the mountain. Bob became the leader, the gentleman, the White Knight. Having figured out how to maneuver the terrain, he is able to lend a hand without being asked or taking away from our own enjoyment of the experience in silence. Bob's grounded strength provides a safer stepping ground for both Karon and me. Neither of us had planned on or expected Bob's assistance, yet since he was taking the lead, it was a more relaxed descent down the mountain.

Angels, a Dream, a Hike and more Angels

~~NOTES~~

Chapter 2

The Fall, Awakening and Rescue

We really don't know why things happen as they do, but they do, and we learn to live with the circumstances, synchronicity, and possibly the truth of it all.

By the time we reach the crag's 20 foot long, 12 inch width ledge, any fear of making it safely across turns into a mystical kind of magic in the air. The three of us have a combined harmony, staying together yet acting independently for whatever needs each of our bodies require. Bob is way ahead. As I enter the precipice, the ledge with Karon behind me, my confidence soars.

I maneuver this ledge the way I had come up, by using the wall of the mountain as support for my back and sidestepping along its path. Whenever I look down I feel the fear of the past, but quickly it turns into a presence of internal power, knowing my feet are planted firmly in every step. At three feet into the ledge my arms are at an angle at my sides and my back and hands flat against the wall of the mountain, moving sideways, looking out over the forest. Since my body is flexible, when I reach the rock that protrudes from the mountain's wall, I move slightly in my midsection/rib area, very slowly, to make room for it and pass it. As my body makes this slight rib movement, I feel my body shifting in a way that is different than I anticipated. I

The Fall, Awakening and Rescue

quickly look down to see my right foot sliding off the ledge.

I am falling. I have a flash thought, "I will turn and grab onto the ledge." As I turned, my eyes wide open, I saw my fingers scratching to hold the dirt and my nails tearing as they tried to grab for the rock's ledge I had just been standing on. My body, still turning, began a flight with the angels, as in my dream the night before. For me, the agreement for silence that day was over! I was screaming! Strangely, I also felt a sense of safety, a "knowing" about what to do. I was not afraid. I was completely conscious. I saw the sky, then, my body turned upside down, seeing the dirt again. About that time I heard Bob and Karon's voices in ethereal oneness say, "we're here, we're here"! This comforted me, while my body made a complete 360-degree turn and I bounced off a rock.

I felt my body falling. I did not have any sensation of pain or fear as I bounced off each rock. It was as if I was flying and completely safe. Like a dream that is so real, I completed the next tossing of my body, and landed on the rocks below, on my back, feeling as if I was being laid down inside God's huge hands. The wind knocked out of my lungs, I was aware of needing to begin taking in air. However, there was a much bigger plan taking precedence over my instinctive desire to be in control.

Lying facing the sun on the rocks of this mountain, in almost a trance state, without an instinctual moment of gasping for air to fill my lungs, I went into an experience of what seemed to be another dimension. I didn't know what to call it. It seemed to have a mysterious life of its own. My body's air felt as if it was being vacuumed out of my belly, and my energy seemed to be escaping with it. From my inner vision, I watched a silver and gold cord—about one inch in diameter—wavering and reaching into the vastness of the universe. It seemed like the electrical cord of my own energy leaving my body and extending to God, and it kept going, and going, and reaching, reaching far out into the universe, while I felt my life force continuously being sucked out of me.

In a flash, I recalled a past memory, a death experience from a past life that involved my children from this life, and I sensed an urgency to return for them. Immediately I spoke aloud, as if waking from a dream, "What an interesting choice of experience." My body's cord, my energy pulsating within it, returned to my belly and began filling me with life force. By this time Karon was at my side, listening, waiting to see what was happening to me.

Karon's concerns were real. She was watching her good friend's face that had been drained of its life force—blue and ashen gray—become filled with life again. And then she heard me say, "I choose to have this experience completely in my body with ease, grace, and joy." As I peeked my eyes open I saw her leaning over me. As if to answer her unspoken question, I said with a breath filled voice, "I'..... m ......OK, ... I'..... m….. O..... K." Karon was relieved, and had already granted me a great gift: being by my side.

The Fall, Awakening and Rescue

Many times in her life Karon had mysteriously been put in situations where she was the only person around who had an ability to help people in crisis. She shared with me at lunch one day about a year after my fall, how this works, when she recalled a particular incident. Karon was at an aquarium with friends visiting the ocean's wonder when all of a sudden she heard a startling crashing noise. Everyone looked in the direction of the crash and Karon could see that one of the tanks had burst and people began running away from the tank's rushing water and flying broken glass. She froze, her body's energy filled with a brilliant golden light and began to run toward the people who may have been injured, without thinking of her own safety.

Glass had flown in all directions, she spied a woman lying on the ground. A piece of glass shard had punctured the woman deep into her forehead. She was still conscious wondering what was happening to her. Karon asked a man close by if she could have the t-shirt he was wearing, and he gladly offered it to assist her. Karon, the golden light energy within and surrounding her, gently commanded the woman to be calm, then assured her that "she would be alright." Once the injured woman saw she was safe, Karon put the t-shirt around the shard, and said in a commanding voice, as she pulled the shard from this woman's forehead "Through the healing power of God, heal this woman."

Kneeling over her with both of her hands on the glass, she extracted the sharp object from deep within the woman's bleeding forehead. Karon stayed with her for a few more minutes, until she knew the woman would be all right. Someone had called the paramedics, and Karon left the scene inconspicuously to re-join her friends, who wondered why she mysteriously disappeared. She went about the rest of her day, seemingly unaffected by the event.

When she was telling me the story, I could believe that such an incomprehensible energy existed within her, and had a feeling of "knowing" this was her truth. Karon and I shared each other's company in a very sacred way that day, and knew our connection was beyond mere friends. We agreed that Karon's grace, in surrendering her own judgments of what others might think of her—to run to someone's aid with such determination—was directed by a force much greater than herself.

Karon went on to explain what happens for her in this type of crisis. When she observes a serious situation occurring, she empties herself of her own personality, identity and ego, and asks God if she is to help this person. When it is God's will, a golden light fills her awareness, and she approaches the person who is allowing God's love and healing. Each time this has happened (prior to her time with me on the mountain), the person was okay when Karon left their side; such as only having their injuries to attend to. This time she would be able to witness my healing.

We wondered if Karon's gift had been transferred to me in that moment on the mountain. The process of healing my body with multiple breaks and internal injuries began while up on that mountain. There was

The Fall, Awakening and Rescue

no one on the mountain to diagnose the extent of my internal or external injuries. The power of God's love was available, and we did not need to know the details . . . not until later.

I felt my body's agreement to Karon's command as she sweetly directed me, "surrender to the experience." Immediately in my inner eye I was submersed within the warm ocean, breathing underwater and floating on my back, when a school of dolphins approached me. The dolphins swam close to my body, touching my back, touching and swimming through my legs and arms. Each time the dolphins touched a part of my body I sensed an adjustment, a healing. I could see inside my body! The many frayed muscles, tendons, and ligaments became smooth and strong. I witnessed my body changing from the inside!

Everywhere the dolphins touched me, I heard and experienced bones snapping gently into place, muscles musically riding the sound waves of health, and replacing themselves with new strength and vitality. The deeper I surrendered, the more light I saw (with closed eyes), and the more sounds I heard. These sounds, lights, and feelings were unknown to me at the time, but I paid attention deeply because something was happening to me that was so powerful it commanded all my attention. The light came through my eyelids from the angels in my dream the night before. I felt safe, protected, no pain or fear, guided by some energy, apparently the God force working within me. I thank God my usually active mind was able to surrender.

50 Feet in 4 Seconds

   My consciousness shifted momentarily to my surroundings. There was commotion, people scurrying around and talking to me. Another moment inside as I scanned my body, I knew I was going to be OK. Thinking to myself, "I'm going to walk down that mountain, not today, but some day not far away." I adjusted my body to be in a more comfortable position on the huge boulders, which were holding me with their strong energy, as the dolphins kept up their gentle, loving healing of my broken body. I instructed some of the hikers that had approached me to help, "Sh, . . Sh, . . Sh. . . Go find my cell phone and call for help." I realized at that moment, that even though their voices were not saying what they were thinking, I could hear what they were thinking loud and clear.

   "Oh my God, she's going to die, how can we help her?" "She is all broken up, what can I do?" "She is going to be crippled for life." Their thoughts were filled with fear out of a genuine concern and desperation to help me. It felt to me as if these words could have landed right on top of me and become true.

   I asked them, (and their thoughts), to leave my side by giving them a job that would distract them, yet make them feel as if they were helping, which was clearly what they intended to do. All of a sudden my consciousness was clear about what people really want in life. What they express in words or what their actions are, is not necessarily what they intend. What people truly want is to be helpful and kind, but their words and thoughts are so often fearful, blameful and even attacking. Unknowingly, these hikers were

The Fall, Awakening and Rescue

actually projecting their beliefs onto me, which I refused to experience. I knew I was healing, but at that time I had to stay inside my own (body's) space, and allow them to express themselves. They really could help, but not in the way they thought they could.

As they went onto their duty, I then brought my attention back inside my body, watching and experiencing fully my sweet dolphins, and sank into a deeper peace while my body continued its healing. I knew what was happening on some level, but having never experienced this before, I was paying close attention. I was watching something amazing happen to me, which I somehow seemed to understand on a purely intuitive level, certainly not in my mind, and it felt good.

Some time later, the hikers came up to me again, and told me they found my cell phone but the battery was gone. They seemed panicked, and that panic was stopping them from doing anything further. With their thoughts blaring inside them, they hesitated and waited for further direction. In my best voice with what breath I could muster, I claimed knowingly, "You will find the battery, slip it on, dial 911, and push send." As if only by my declaration, it seemed seconds later that they found the battery, attached it to the phone, and the emergency call was made. I was surprised by my commanding words. I was taking authority, responsibility for my health and well being, and accepting the love of God working within me. I began directing, even coaching the people around me for what was in my best interest.

Then Bob appeared on my left side asking if he could do anything. Bob, unlike the stray hikers, was able to understand and hear what I needed, without any fear thoughts or judgments directing him. He had been doing some very deep healing work with crystals from the earth, so his natural tendency was to get behind me, and put his hands toward my head to add a flow of healing energy toward me. I felt the energy press into my head immediately, and said "Too much." So he backed up and still it was too much. I asked him to go for help, and he was off—down the mountain like a deer—graceful and assured. He found a jeep driver with a radio, and they also called 911. That call from the jeep driver and my found cell phone, came within five minutes of each other.

   I responded to the questions from the hikers and Karon with a gentle confidence, and assured them that I would be alright, but this was different for me. I had not known myself to be so confident when I was in such a vulnerable state. Usually anytime I was hurt or felt weak in any way I would cower inside myself, and allow people who wanted to help me do whatever they knew to do, as if they knew better than I did. This time, my experience inside my body was like watching a most magnificent light and sound show directed by the universe. It gave me a sense of pure power. I knew I would be rescued, and that I would be fine.

   What I really wanted was to pay attention to the messages I was receiving inside my body, albeit from a source which I had never known before. When someone asked me something I responded very clearly

The Fall, Awakening and Rescue

like I knew what I was talking about, and this felt right to me, but I wondered "How did I switch to this confident self? I did not have to work on it, or train myself, or reveal anything or transform anything; I just did it!"

There were several notable events that happened in the year prior to this hike. With some time passing and as I write these pages I give much reflection to "who was I that brought this experience to me?"

In the Spring of 1996 I was invited to attend a gathering of about 18 people interested in being ordained in the order of Melchizedek. Without time to think it through (in those days I would ponder a decision for days), I agreed to be there with much enthusiasm, as if I knew I was going to participate in something very special. The ordination took place on a beautiful Sunday on Bell Rock with a bit of a chill in the morning, warming towards noon, which was the actual time the ordinations began. Dan Chesbro, as far as I know and am told, is the only person alive today that is gifted with the benediction into the Melchizedek priesthood and can ordain others.

In early 1986, Dan was guided to "call the priests." He was clear he was not allowed to ask anyone to become a priest, somehow people found him, nor was he allowed to turn anyone away. The decision to become a priest through the Sanctuary of the Beloved, his organization, and to participate in the ordination ceremony was to be a personal choice, one made with God. Dan sometimes jokes about the fact that this is the only religious order in the world with well over

3,000 priests and no congregation. Many priests choose to continue in their current careers and demonstrate the Light of unconditional love to their best ability in all matters.

The blossoming of the Order of Melchizedek seems to be a result of cellular memory of the Christ within being activated. There are several Biblical references to share in this writing. They are taken from Hebrews, a letter written by an unnamed Christian in AD 85-95.

"He is first, by translation of his name, king of righteousness, and then he is also king of Salem, that is king of peace. He is without father or mother or genealogy and has neither beginning of days or end of life, but resembling the Son of God he continues a priest for ever." (Hebrews 7:2-3)

This seems to indicate that Melchizedek is an immortal being and honored as the king of peace. Jesus, often called the prince of peace, is connected to Melchizedek in the following passages.

"This becomes even more evident when another priest arises in the likeness of Melchizedek, who has become a priest, not according to a legal requirement concerning bodily descent, but by the power of an indestructible life. For it is witnessed of him: Thou art a priest for ever after the Order of Melchizedek." (Hebrews 7:15-17)

"We have this as a sure and steadfast anchor of the soul, a hope that enters into the inner shrine behind the curtain, where Jesus has gone as a forerunner on our behalf, having become a

The Fall, Awakening and Rescue

high priest forever after the order of Melchizedek." (Hebrews 6:19-20)

The indication is that Jesus was a priest after Melchizedek, not because of the laws of the people but because of God's law.

I was asked to wear white and be in meditation to be open to receive any information that would pertain to my life's path. I was also instructed to be willing to sacrifice something very significant in my life, an offering to God in exchange for my receiving these vows of an ancient teaching, something that either has been hard for me to give up or that I had been wanting to give up for a long time. Choosing was stressful, I thought, "just the right thing", "something that made a big difference for me", "something that would equal a divine gift from God." Pondering for sometime and with trepidation, willing yet untrusting that I could do it, I chose to stop smoking.

During the following six months, integrating the ordination as a Melchizedek priestess took me into several different realms exploring the esoteric teachings I longed to learn. At this time in my life I realized it was time for me to let go of my rigid past behaviors of thinking that I had to do only what others wanted of or for me. It was time to get out there and really follow what interested me.

I chose learning to communicate with the angels. I became so engulfed in learning everything I could about them, reading and asking questions of people that already had been working with them: it was all I wanted to do. Periodically, I began to hear some uncertain noises and see some quick flashes of colors and light pass in my peripheral vision. Also, I practiced asking questions to the angels wondering when I would hear something from them. I started to feel very close to them even though I could prove nothing, my senses felt them around me and I was enjoying learning directly from them. I rarely mentioned this to anyone as I was not sure how people would react and coming from my past where most everything I did seemed wrong to the people around me, I did not want to risk others criticism. The angels taught me they loved us so much and wanted to help us learn to be more conscious and loving towards each other. I learned that they grew as we grew and each time we asked them for help *they* actually would evolve another level. I learned they watched us all the time and waited for our questions or acknowledgement in some way, so they could be of service to us, and how it pleased them so when we did ask, then thank them. The angels became my new love affair, endearing themselves to me with each interaction. It was a true mutual admiration affair.

On January 2, 1997, I remember resting on my couch in the afternoon after having many ceremonies celebrating the beginning of the New Year the day before. Suddenly and spontaneously I heard an unfamiliar otherworldly voice swell within my body that was loud and strong. This voice said, "You are a precious child of God" to my Being. Immediately I began to cry realizing that in my life I had never had

The Fall, Awakening and Rescue

one thought like that for myself. I began forgiving myself for the thoughts I did have, the familiar harshness of the mind that I lived with daily. I kept forgiving every single thought I had for about a week, until I was complete.

About one month before I fell I had a vision while watching the re-release of *The Empire Strikes Back*. Anticipating my favorite part of the movie—the introduction and message of Yoda, I was disappointed that I did not get to see it. Instead, I was lifted out of my body and shown a vision of myself standing in front of thousands of people with my arms wildly, passionately waving, and my heart pounding as I spoke my heart's words. "It is time for us to 'Just Do It,'" like the Nike slogan. "Do what we are here to do! Do what we are meant to do! Do what we feel right to do! Do not hold back any longer, or wait for anything, anyone or some day. Just do it, NOW!"

Almost synchronistic, two days before my hike I was in a day long class to learn conscious language. I learned that the Hopi Indians native tongue had no past or future tenses, they spoke only from the moment, without time constricting them. This class of mastery of language taught me to upgrade my words, be creative and as such raise my personal frequency. I also learned that many of our habitual phrases to express ourselves actually bring us harm and stop us from having our dreams, because our language states that good things we experience are "unbelievable." There were many other nuances of our language I learned, so much so, that the next day I choose to keep silent, to review my mental vocabulary, which kept me stuck and feeling small. I realized I had a box for my words, in this box were the only words I ever used, all the time. I expressed myself the same way, in many different situations. I began to open this box and the dictionary became my best friend. This is why I requested a silent hike with my friends, to learn more about what goes on inside my own head while doing regular, everyday activities.

Back on the mountain, I only had one thought that interrupted the flow of this beautiful natural Godly energy, which was "How will I pay for these injuries?" An answer came immediately from the energy source still circulating within me. "Don't worry." I felt somehow comforted, and I trusted those words instinctively. Being present to what was happening in my body, and allowing all the scurrying around outside of me, was different for me. Typically for me, I would be "out there" with them trying to help, (ridiculous, isn't it?), and distracting myself from the experience. This time I felt I was learning something I had prayed for most of my life. Something that was answering the questions I had asked myself since I was a little girl: "Why am I here?" and "Who am I?"

The rescue team finally arrived up the mountain with approximately 18 people, including the Emergency Medical Technicians, the Sedona Fire Department, and a group called Ropes That Rescue, bringing with them a lot of equipment to carry up that steep grade. They were prepared for anything. When they reached me, I spoke to them and answered all the medical questions

The Fall, Awakening and Rescue

they had as best I could. As soon as they knew I was alive and conscious, they immediately began an IV saline solution and prepared me for the intense trip down the mountain. There were 22 of them counting the hikers, and Bob and Karon who had joined in. I watched them for a while, but as soon as I knew they could be completely trusted with my safety, I went back inside my body, into the state of bliss and surrender to the experience.

I am on a gurney. The team takes great care to ready themselves in concert with each other around me for the steep grade downhill, making sure their footing is secure. They magnificently orchestrate themselves close together while they hand me down one person at a time performing a "caterpillar chain." Once the injured party is on the stretcher and the team is standing shoulder-to-shoulder (just like the angels did in my dream), they hand the gurney down, one hand at a time. The top team member carefully moves to the bottom of the stretcher, then all hands move one hand-down again, and another team member from the top rotates to the bottom of the stretcher. All of this is done slowly and very carefully, as there are many loose rocks, soft dirt, and forest under their feet.

Once on the flat surface, the team is riding the edge of another cliff and we begin to hear, and then see the helicopter. The helicopter pilot had the finesse of years of flying. He brought the helicopter in at a slant, with just enough room to clear his blades from the mountain's wall, and to land the helicopter on a ledge nearby. Many people around me were saying that he could not accomplish this. At one point, I overheard the ground team leader on the radio with the pilot instructing him on where and how to land. Besides the difficult landing, his regard for nature in his response to "Be careful of the yucca," was music to my ears. I would not have been happy if a tree had to be damaged for me to be rescued. Everyone was amazed to watch this highly trained pilot land on the shallow ledge. They watched with even more awe, as they saw him maneuver his take off with me safely tucked inside.

All the while I was hearing words of comfort from a voice inside me that was so strong, I honored it with my full attention. This powerful yet soft voice was undeniably reassuring to me. In the past, I would have had many concerns about my safety and survival in such a traumatic situation. My own mind would have destructively traumatized me. However, this voice was so strong and profound I let go into the blissful and reassured feelings, watching my body continue to heal, while trusting the rescue team.

The Fall, Awakening and Rescue

~~NOTES~~

Chapter 3

<u>The Hospital, Surgery and Miracle Healing</u>

Miracles are happening all the time.
All you have to do is pay attention.

When I arrived at the hospital emergency room, I was in and out of a blissful nurturing state. When asked a question I answered, then promptly closed my eyes to shield the overhead lights, and returned to bliss again. They told me I was going in and out of consciousness. I felt as though I was very sharp answering all their questions. I remember my clothes being cut off my body to properly assess my injuries. I was wearing a brand new white t-shirt, with a gold Flower of Life emblem on the front that day. The Flower of Life symbol is a sacred geometric pattern that represents consciously being in and part of everything in the universe. What a metaphor for what I experienced that truly sacred day.

As I continuously surrendered to this powerful experience, the magnificent team of doctors, nurses, and technicians readied me for surgery on my right arm. I overheard someone say that my bones were sticking out and were broken in many places. Without concern or worry clouding my mind, I "knew" that everything that was happening was in perfect order, for my ultimate healing.

The Hospital, Surgery and Miracle Healing

My surgeon Dr. Timothy Bonatus, introduced himself to me and told me I was being prepared for surgery. Next, the doctor's assistant introduced herself. Then Dr. Lee, the Anesthesiologist, introduced himself. While they were all standing over me, to my surprise these words popped out of my mouth. I said, "I would like to speak to all of you before I go into surgery." They agreed, but it did not happen. I was put deeply to sleep within seconds. Feeling a slight twinge of disappointment as I drifted off, I had yet another new experience in that moment. I had total trust for their expertise and knowledge, and let go of my desire to speak to them.

Ten days later when I saw Dr. Bonatus in his office, I directly mentioned my disappointment at not being able to speak to the team prior to surgery. My intent to speak was to let them know I understood that they were skilled physicians and to ask them to treat me as though I was alive, healed, and grateful for their service. What happened was that my intent got carried out without speaking. My doctor's response to me that day was that I spoke quite a lot during surgery! I sensed he was teasing me, and he would not say what I had said. We giggled and smiled at each other, and I did not ask him to tell me what I had said. I felt from his communication that he had heard me say things he didn't understand how to fit into his world.

After surgery, I was told I had 22 broken bones: my left foot in the arch/heel/ankle, right foot/ankle/leg, three places in my pelvis (right, center, left), my right scapula, a compound fracture in my right arm, and a large bump in my head which took several stitches. My right arm required surgery and placement of a six-inch metal plate and nine screws.

Stan, my recent ex-husband (we ended our marriage two years prior to preserve our friendship), was in Intensive Care with me as I awakened. He sat in a chair by my bedside day and night throughout the entire weekend to ensure my rest and provide whatever I needed. He only dozed when I slept.

My friends came in later that afternoon and brought stuffed animals with the healing energy of Reiki embedded in them, flowers, crystals, music, essential oils, and most of all, their love. They started calling me "Miracle Woman" as I shared some of the stories I had experienced so far. Each one shared with me about the prayer chain they had created on my behalf. This prayer chain reached and connected every corner of the world together with focused energy of healing for me. Every element in my room provided some form of healing vibration that was of a healing nature, including everyone's feelings, words and attitudes towards my healing body. Some of my friends had shared the conscious language class with me, so their expression and chosen words were delightful to my ears. They thought only positive thoughts, made me laugh, and we giggled as they shared their hospital stories. I remember getting a few phone calls. One was from my sister and one I remember was from a teacher/friend, Vonn, who taught the conscious language class I was in just two days before and was teaching me how to use essential oils for healing. As soon as she heard about

The Hospital, Surgery and Miracle Healing

my fall she called Gary Young the owner and visionary of *Young Living Essential Oils* to find out what oils were best to heal my body. He responded: helichrysm and lavender - so my friends quickly brought them into my room to be used daily.

Early Sunday morning when I awoke, I kept feeling an odd sensation. Something was happening that my conscious mind did not understand. My room was quiet, no one was there, so I meditated on my body and the energy I was feeling. I was engaged with a powerful feeling. The movement of this energy within me was healing me so fast it appeared to have an intelligence all of its own.

At the same time I felt a very different energy moving through me. This energy seemed to have a much different force, a counter-expression so to speak, or an opposition to the healing energy. There was definitely a constriction and a more sluggish feeling within it. I immediately noticed the difference and it became clear to me that this odd feeling energy was beginning to hinder my body's own healing process. I wanted to understand it more.

A few minutes later the nurse came in for my morning check in. I said to her, "Why am I so groggy?" She quickly replied, "You are on morphine." I was shocked, and questioned why. She answered in a "matter of fact" tone, "Because you are in excruciating pain!"

I was appalled at her assumption of knowing how I felt and replied adamantly and with a bit of sarcasm, "I AM?" Quietly, I realized that was the sluggishness I

50 Feet in 4 Seconds

was feeling. Almost interrupting I requested, "Please take me off of it." She explained she was just following rules and had to speak to the doctor to see if he would change the order. She quickly added that the doctor would not be available for a while, that he was "on call" and could be anywhere. I pled to speak to him as soon as possible. Almost simultaneously, I had another strange feeling. It was a "knowing" that my doctor was *in* the building, and it would not take her long to reach him. I relaxed into that knowing while she located him.

Sometime later, it came to me how I knew he was in the building. I "knew" and could *feel his energy*. Yes, the night before during my surgery he was in my *energy fields*. When she told me the doctor was not available I was listening intently to her speak, and, at the same time, somehow my energy fields scanned the building for his presence there. I felt his distinct presence on one of the upper floors, and I "knew." This "knowing" when the nurse and I were speaking came as natural to me as knowing my ABCs.

When the doctor came in to see me an hour later, I asked him if he had been in the building. He said, "Yes." Without any further discussion about his whereabouts, (I had been validated of my "knowing") he explained the importance of the morphine almost exactly as the nurse had explained it to me.

He reluctantly told me he would take me off the morphine if I promised to let him know the minute I felt any pain. I promised him if there were any pain, he would be the first to know. I felt he was speaking to me as if he thought I was being tough, which was so very

The Hospital, Surgery and Miracle Healing

far from the truth. I slept great that night and watched that sluggish energy melt into the beautiful energy that was healing me.

As I had expressed on the mountain, I would have this experience in ease, grace, and joy, completely conscious in body, mind and spirit. The evidence was clear this was happening in every interaction I was having.

To my astonishment, even the hospital staff offered themselves only when absolutely necessary: As when taking blood pressure, changing antibiotic fluids, bringing food into the room, taking me to the bathroom, etc. They took special care to be respectful of my space yet responsive, thoughtful and considerate of my wishes at the same time. I was In-Joy at what I was experiencing.

When an aide, the doctor or a nurse came into my room that was negative, I felt the grace within me, and responded to him or her from that energy. It was as if I could actually change the energy I felt from them into healing energy if it did not match mine. I wasn't trying to do this, but to my pleasant surprise it just kept happening, and I kept noticing. By Monday night, a nurse was offering to "spritz" me with lavender oil and water, before I went to sleep. During the day my friends had sprayed me while visiting, both to provide the healing qualities of the oil and to give a fresh scent to my room.

The staff even considered my wishes when making arrangements to have my bathroom fixed. A nurse asked, "Would you prefer during the night or in the morning?" I responded, "In the morning," and, "If I need to use the bathroom tonight, is there something else that could be used?"

She immediately brought in a portable potty-chair on wheels. I was being treated with love and care. This time in the hospital was so very different from my past experiences, when I got jabbed, intruded upon, told what I had to do, was forced to take things I did not request, and on and on and on. It felt so good that this kind treatment was happening now.

Experiencing this, I realized how we create our lives. If we always relate to everything in the moment as something that has happened in the past, (by saying something like, "I know this one" or "I know how this goes") then the moment does not exist. The moment is controlled by the past—in fact it "is" the past. Being in the present moment is living life to its fullest, now.

Several miracles happened on Monday. Starting off at about 7:30 am when Dr. Bonatus came in and asked how I was feeling. He had a speculative look on his face that I read to mean, he was expecting me to complain about being in pain. He was surprised to hear my response, which was, "Great! How are you this fine morning?" The look on his face was precious, and nothing that could compare with what was to come next. I was the one surprised this time!

Quickly letting go of his astonishment about me not needing any more drugs, he told me he had seen something on the MRI that was taken prior to my surgery on Saturday night. He told me I had to have surgery on my right leg too! However, he wanted to

The Hospital, Surgery and Miracle Healing

verify this again, by taking another x-ray to see what it looked like today. About an hour after taking the second x-ray the doctor came in with yet another totally bewildered look on his face. I interpreted this to mean something like . . . what he was about to report to me had yet another dimension outside of his experience and expertise. He told me that he looked at the x-ray and it was OK! Miraculously, I would not need another surgery. He also said that I apparently had only 9 bones left to heal! Even I was astounded to hear *that* report.

Stan had witnessed the exchange with the doctor. I looked at him with that familiar sense that couples have with each other and exclaimed, "See, I'm already healed!" and he got it. The doctor not knowing what to make of our exchange casually moved to the next order of business; to inform me he had to cast my left leg. I asked him how long I would be in the cast. His response of four to six weeks was expected. I responded, "One."

He said teasingly, "If you do that I'll write a report about you."

I said emphatically, "Get out your pen." *(His report is the forward to his book!)*

I was beginning to understand what was taking place in my experience, in my body. I knew what my friends had said the day before was true. I was a "Miracle Woman", and it had nothing to do with my former self. This was God, inside of me, making every bit of this wonderful and magnificent transformation possible.

My previous experiences in a hospital where I was the patient were so different. Usually I would be the one to ask the silly questions, playing a victim to my own illness or malady. This time I felt positive I knew what I was saying, and could see myself healed very soon. This self-assured feeling was not coming from the old me that I knew, but at the same time, I felt very sure about it.

Our reality was shifting in each moment to a new reality—one that has the body feeling empowered to self-heal. My doctor was getting the message with me in that moment. What he had known in his past experience of healing was all based on his education, knowledge, and personal experience of treating human beings—and very predictable. What he and the rest of us were learning was that the human spirit and body's consciousness have only one agenda and that is to be healthy, vital, fully alive, and healthy. Instinctually, even automatically, the body will keep aligning itself towards this ultimate goal, regardless of your consciousness or circumstances. The Divine plan is already set in motion, and you are showing up every day to fulfill that plan. Given the choice, my role is to experience being the best I can be in every way, to surrender to the Spirit within. For I, together with my Spirit, am ultimately responsible for my own healing.

As a child I had always known that I could heal myself. I remember a hot summer when I was about five years old. My mother took my sisters and me out for our usual walk after dinner. I was eating a popsicle while walking. My mother was pushing my two sisters

The Hospital, Surgery and Miracle Healing

in a stroller. One of my sisters was about 2 years old then, began to get upset with me about something and I felt an unfriendly energy coming toward me. I suddenly fell off the edge of the curb I was walking along, and the popsicle stick jabbed down my throat. My mother quickly picked me up and ran carrying me into the house and told me she would take care of me. She thought that by putting this purple stuff in my throat I would feel better. I knew that the purple stuff would only mask the real healing, and that I could heal myself even though I could not tell my mother that.

At that age, I simply did not have the ability to express what I knew. How could a five-year-old communicate, "I know how to heal myself," and have a mother understand it? My mother was the authority, and I trusted her so I let her wishes override my internal knowing. From that experience, I formed a belief that I wouldn't be recognized or valued if I healed myself. Therefore, resistance got locked into my body. That resistance lodged deeper into my being with each experience of pain or illness, until now.

In the hospital, I realized that the doctors were there as guides, and can actually only do so much. Self-healing (through our God-self), left to its own resources and natural processes, is what the body will do naturally. It is the mind that interjects thoughts in a way that can hinder this beautiful process.

~~NOTES~~

Chapter 4

<u>Home Recovery with Angels</u>

In the end, love is the only medicine that can heal the wounds of the world. In the universe, it is love that binds everything together. Love is the very foundation, beauty, and fulfillment of life. If we dive deep enough into ourselves, we will find that the one thread of Universal love ties all beings together. As this awareness dawns within us, all dis-harmony will cease. Abiding peace alone will reign.
Quote on sign in Ammachi's Ashram San Ramon, Ca.

On Tuesday morning, day three in the hospital, the physical therapist visited and gave me instructions to get ready to leave the hospital. Dr. Bonatus must have shared my improvement and asked her to administer the next steps for me. She said I could leave on Wednesday if I walked to the bathroom, and had a bowel movement (neither of which had I done to this point). The challenge came, and I was ready for it. I had an appointment with her around noon.

My children arrived in my room that morning. My daughter, Kim, then 27, flew in from Hawaii where she lives, and my son, Tod, then 24, flew in from California where he lives. My children, responsible for their own lives, weren't sure what to expect when they saw me. They had received a call from Stan prior to his seeing me, and he relayed his concerns to them. They immediately put themselves on a plane in fear that I might be dead, or have brain damage or irreversible damage to my body.

They somberly walked into my hospital room afraid of what they might see. My friends and I greeted them with love and smiles. Relieved to see me in good spirits, they shared their fears with me, and expressed concerns for my well-being. Within an hour of their arrival, their stress was alleviated in time to witness and help me with my next challenge, getting ready to leave the hospital after only three days. They vowed to stay with me as long as I needed them and to help in whatever way they could.

The physical therapist left a quad walker in my room to use for getting to the bathroom. It was my first attempt out of bed, on my own. Carefully, I eased on to the edge of the bed, using my left arm for balance, pushing up off the bed. I realized I required a strong arm to assist me, asked my son for his arm, then carefully made my move. Sliding off the edge of the bed I suddenly remembered I had training as a dancer. As my feet landed on the floor, I used my creativity and dancer's awareness. I stepped down on my heel then balanced on my other heel. Then with momentary balance, I turned my toes toward the bathroom, balanced again, then heels followed—like a scoot step, that was danced in the 50's to get from one side of the dance floor to the other.

Later that day at my session with the physical therapist, she laughed when I told her about my creative way to get to the bathroom. She said she would prefer me to walk in the normal way, forward, heel-toe, heel-toe. She encouraged me to walk in this way as much as possible so no new bad habits were created and the mind and body would remember exactly how to walk with grace. She took me into the physical therapy room and showed me how to walk up a step about one inch high and then down again. I thought, "Piece of cake, only one inch!" Not! My body began to sweat profusely and was moving very slowly and carefully as I approached the step. She talked me through each muscle's movement.

"Oy!" I thought. I learned how to use the crutches for support, and how to be in walking mode so my body would remember how it would heal moving naturally. I did it! With that accomplished my motivation was high, and successfully achieved their other requirement for discharge on Wednesday morning. I was on my way home—to heal.

When I arrived home there were people waiting for me, like a welcoming family. As we pulled into my driveway I noticed a wheelchair ramp from the driveway to the front doorstep. Someone said that Stan had arranged it and set it up for me before he left for his pre-arranged trip to visit his homeland, South Africa. Three days in the hospital seemed like a lifetime, so when I was wheeled up the ramp into my home I asked to stop on the porch for a moment.

I closed my eyes, took in a huge breath and smelled the fresh spring air filled with aliveness. I felt like I had died and been reborn. Three days ago I thought I was going on a hike, I did not know I was taking a journey!

As I was wheeled on the pathway to my front door, I saw my beautiful indigo colored irises in full bloom. The rosemary bush on the front lawn, which was really a pebble patch, trailed down the wall's side and filled the air with its woodsy scent. I was elated to be in an environment of love in my own home. I lived alone at this time, but you would not have known it by the number of people always at my house showing up to help me.
   Sheila, a nurse turned massage therapist, was one angel, who was traveling through town and needed a driveway big enough to park her RV for her stay. I offered mine; she thought she would be about a week. When she heard what had happened to me, she changed her plans to be available to help me as long as I needed her. She said she would cook, clean—anything. She ended up helping for three weeks.
   Then there was Anita, my dear sweet friend who is more like a sister to me. She looks just like an angel with white shiny hair, huge light brown twinkling eyes, and the softest voice of a goddess. I missed my own sisters and family since I had moved to Sedona, especially now. Anita did the grocery shopping, made sure my pain medication was filled—even though I assured her I would not use it, (I never did)--and helped change my clothes before bed.
   DD, the giggling cherub, was one who surprised me daily. She would call me every morning around nine o'clock and ask me if I needed anything. She is so dear to my heart! Before I could answer, she would say, "I'm coming over in about an hour, OK?" I always said

"OK," whether I knew why or not. She could always be counted on to create something fun and useful, like walking in my house with a homemade casserole and salad for lunch.

The first few moments home sitting in the wheelchair, I watched my friends scurry around my kitchen doing things for me, none of which I felt I needed. It was odd being in a place of complete peace within, and really not wanting for anything. I was content to be home, but I began to feel bound watching them. They are in my kitchen looking around for utensils, being useful and laughing, and I'm in a wheelchair! A sort of strange reality struck a chord within me.

Sitting watching this scene, something said to me, "This has all the confinements of me never walking again." My body felt the pangs of constriction, and I knew instinctively I had to do something different. I caught the eye of Sheila and DD, and motioned with my finger for them to come over to me. I asked them to help me out of that wheelchair and put it away, out of my sight. They never questioned my choice. They asked me where I would like to be. I said, "Help me get to the couch. That is where I will heal." I then asked them to please remove the ramp, the walker, and any other equipment that was brought over for my use; though very sweet and thoughtful, I will walk! They helped me up and placed me on my couch.

My friends were all amazing. Before I said or even felt that I was hungry, someone handed me a beautifully prepared sandwich. Before I even thought of using the bathroom, be it toilet or shower, someone offered to escort me there. "Yes" was the only appropriate answer to everything. In the past, my first response to so much attention would have been, "No thank you, I can do it myself." This undeserving attitude was not available in this healing body. I kept changing, continuously thinking differently than I had ever thought before. This body felt like a baby—brand new—learning to live life with loving people around, and accepting their love without question or obligation.

As I reflect now, this situation was very similar to my rebirthing experience in Mexico six months prior to the fall when I finally completed my commitment, my sacrifice, to becoming a Melchizedek priestess.

The weekend of my birthday four of my girlfriends and I were invited to a mutual friend's wedding in Puerto Penasco, Mexico. We drove there in six hours from Sedona and we rented a condo for our weekend getaway. I promised myself this was the weekend I would quit smoking, without telling anyone. I purchased two packs of herbal cigarettes, just to have on hand and begin removing the nicotine from my body. Turned out I never smoked even one of them. Just before midnight of my birthday we were sitting around talking about our life's changes and the conversation came around to a focus on me. They were gently prodding my past, my parents, childhood and before I knew it I was lying on the floor being re-birthed. They were in a circle over me guiding me through a new experience of being born into a family that wanted me, couldn't wait to see me, teach me in a gentle way, watch me grow into a beautiful girl then woman with their encouragement, reassurance, and unconditional love. I never knew this kind of healing existed. It was a very powerful and moving experience for me. The weekend was extraordinary and these four women are still my dearest friends. I stopped smoking and received unconditionally loving parents. I could breathe in new life into those beautiful lungs of mine.

~~NOTES~~

Chapter 5

<u>**Learning Divine Skills**</u>

No one, no matter what is done to you, where you are, what you experience, what you feel or think, what others think or say about you, can take your freedom from you.

A new awareness was that any old thoughts or beliefs I had from the past could not exist in the "present now." Any old patterning, conditioning or points of view that came up, just as rapidly disappeared. Repeating of old thoughts seemed to melt away without trying or wishing them gone. I felt completely peaceful, full of bliss within myself. I wanted for nothing, having everything I could ever need.

This feeling was new, as if I was a baby and did not consciously know what "new" meant. I was having the experience of new, in the now, consciously. I didn't even think of relishing it or extending it unnaturally, like I could capture it and savor it. It was as pure as each moment, fresh and alive, vital and aware, with nothing and everything, all conscious.

Every few hours someone else came over to ask if they could be of help. One day, after several weeks of this, I asked a few people who came over "Are you guys organizing yourselves a schedule to watch over me?" Their united reply was, "No, we are taking care of our lives, and YOU are part of our life." I heard a voice in my head say *"this is harmony."* A wave of happiness spread throughout my body and my heart filled with tears of joy.

While my friends were busy in the kitchen, I became curious about this subtle voice I had been hearing. Where did this voice come from? Who was it? Will it come back again? These questions came and went very quickly, because at the moment I could not grasp a question long enough for an answer to come from my ego mind or past experiences. It seemed that my usual questioning mind would not get answers any longer, at least not the answers I was used to hearing. For some strange reason, as inquisitive as I lived my life, this was fine with me now. In the past, unanswered questions would provoke me to irritation. This must be what surrender is. Since I accepted that as my state of awareness on the mountain, it seemed to be the new context of my life.

My friends' expression of harmony felt so good in my new body that it felt like pure love. Their actions were so unselfish, yet at the same time self-full. (Self-full is explained in more detail in Chapter 13.) My friends were taking care of their own lives first, then coming over to see what I might need to help me take care of me. I felt that I had never heard anything so beautiful expressed before.

After about two weeks I did hear consciously some old self-centered thoughts say, "I could take advantage of this generosity" and I immediately felt tense in my body. I saw in a quick flash, that if I did take advantage I would become dependent on them, and they would very soon resent me. The relationships would suffer and so would I, as in so many past relationships. That subtle voice kept telling me that I could be different, that I could really change, being happier now than ever before, and this was my opportunity. So I began taking a really good look at my answers when someone asked me if I wanted something. Rather than having an automatic answer be "Yes" or "No," I looked honestly to see if I could do it myself, or if I wanted help. I began to choose every word very carefully.

New questions rather than old responses came to me: Would it support me to do it myself? Would I truly love them to support me? Which way would I feel really good? This was such a different way for me. At that moment my body relaxed knowing I could choose another way: a way that would empower me! That tension I felt just moments before, disappeared. I had access to my truth. My body confirmed my inner truth with an unmistakable feeling that I now know would serve me with future questions that arise in my life.

This feeling gave me another insight in that moment about learning to balance my male and female sides. It seemed so automatic that my male side, the protector, aggressor and doer, had taken over without me making the choice, in the past. It was always a reaction, from the past. Embodying my feminine side in this healing space of surrender, I realized how often I had operated out of my male side and now I am making a different choice. This insight turned into a mountainous uncovering of past beliefs, switched gender roles and learning to embrace my feminine goddess within in a way that included grace. Many times I would see myself doing something out of a past belief or structure and come into clarity on what side of me—masculine or feminine—was in control. I would choose again in that moment and learn something new and different for myself and possibly those around me.

Choosing to be consciously responsible about my past choices, my mind's chatter became loud and obvious. My body was also talking to me as well as showing me another truth I could live, not the made up ego-based survival version I had been living. I was listening—listening to my body—realizing that the misunderstandings I had with people in the past, were really my own misunderstandings of my self, mind, body, and emotions. This is one of the illusions of life: believing your own thoughts as if they are real, then relating to the world like your thoughts are true and everyone believes the same as you do.

I learned so much by watching my friends and listening to them. When they came over to see me and care for me, I saw and experienced a different kind of friendship than I had previously—with the same people. They came with no agenda except to be at my side and serve me. They were dedicated to being by my side and learning from the experience with me. My previous thoughts about taxing their lives while caring for me seemed ridiculous in this nurturing and loving energy. We were co-creating an experience, which was a shift in consciousness—one that had everyone in full awareness—by letting go of preconceived notions of what the progress of healing looks like, or should be like. One that gave humanity acceptance of being

Learning Divine Skills

greater than our minds could imagine. Being around this energy gave us insight and new dimension into what we formerly called our "normal" world. I am convinced now "normal" only means "habitual." It is something we do over and over, and have expectations of the results always being the same. In some new pop-psychology teachings I have heard something similar with one variation. Doing the same thing over and over and expecting different results, this is called insanity. So, is "normal" sane or insane?

Meditation came easy at this time. I remember years of practicing meditation with my will, before giving in to the mind's continual chatter and quitting. Now, the silence lent itself to see myself, and my life as I had known it, but different. I saw the life I had as an illusion conceived by my imagination, manufactured by a fear-filled child to keep me safe, protected, and secure in what I thought I knew. The energy in the silence while healing was clearly God's message to me that I sit up and take notice, that I listen more and think less.

That I would see the Truth if I eliminated my mind's designs and allowed God's agreement with my soul to surface through this body's experience of life. The more I breathed into my body the easier it was to let go and stay in silence, in the safety of God's loving arms. Dialoguing with my body at night became a quiet, meditative, sacred healing practice. Even though some nights I would be awake all night, in the morning I felt rested and alert.

The first few nights home from the hospital I was awake four days and four nights. On the first night I was curious. On the second night I was angry. As the anger built inside me, I felt myself getting angrier and angrier. I let go of the anger towards myself and began learning to change my old patterned thoughts about sleeping. I used to think if I did not sleep well I would be tired all the next day, or that I would have to make up the sleep somehow. I asked myself, for the first time, questions about why I'm thinking this way. I thought I was losing something if I did not sleep well. "Am I losing something?" I realized these thoughts were part of my past thinking, and to my surprise I easily let them go. I would sail through the days and nights, realizing I was being taught important life lessons and journeying to learn why I am here, and who I really am—things I had hungered to have answered my entire life. Later, I realized that if I applied this "choose what you are thinking" technique to change my thinking mind, I would change quicker.

The process began. I heard the voice inside me say, *"What angers you?"*

I answer, "That I have to be up, when resting would be a healthier way to heal."

A response came, "You think this is the way to heal?" "Yes." "What if there is another way?"

I say, "OK show me."

Immediately I am taken on a journey inside my body. I mean literally, my eyes turned inside my head, I saw my brain, its parts, color, size, shape, texture, exactly what it looked like anatomically, and I was intrigued to learn more. Instantly a pain came from my ankle. My eyes, breath, and conscious attention

Learning Divine Skills

directed me to my ankle. My mind wanting to know and understand this process began chattering. For some reason I said to my mind (or maybe it wasn't me), "Watch this process and learn." I was amazed to learn that sacred love dwells inside the innate wisdom of each cell in my body.

I turn to deep breathing and prayer, knowing that God and my angels are guiding and protecting me. In my solar plexus I recognize that old scared feeling of "What's happening to me?" My body lays perfectly still, my eyes closed and the depth of night draws me deeper into my body. I am drawn to a broken part. Again, it is my ankle. The closer I get to the aching pain the more it becomes tremendous, unbearable pain. Instead of writhing and tossing around in anger, I surrender and feel the sensations.

My mind is suddenly quiet. I am intently listening for the next direction. I hear, *"Do you want to know the story of the past, how you originally got a broken ankle?"* "Yes." I am immediately transported to a country setting, dirt road, dried out brush, a few trees and barren land. I'm being dragged tied to a horse, down a rocky dirt road. The ankle that is broken now is the one tied to the rope. I feel the pain of being dragged, and it does not seem like there will be any stopping. Along the road I see a small tree coming up on my right, I grab onto it causing a pulling action between my right arm and my left leg. I am now stretched by the horses pulling me and holding onto the tree when snap, my shoulder and right arm are now broken. As I let go of the tree my right arm dangles behind me, still being dragged.

Now in my body, both my left ankle and right arm are in horrific pain. As I moved through this process I learned that when the mind is not concerned for its survival or safety, the body's inner wisdom is revealed. When a pain is felt without being in fear, the mind could ask intelligent questions and begin to have a new understanding of how everything affects our consciousness, our environment, and our bodies. When my left ankle and right arm pain became so severe in that conscious-unconscious theta state, I was able to "be with" the pain.

   I then asked, "What may I learn from this pain?" It seemed as if this pain was actually speaking with me, and the response came, *"During this time you were loved dearly, but your exceptional awareness threatened the community you lived in,"* said the inner voice. The next picture was made clear to me. *"You were considered very intuitive by some, and their reliance upon you usurped the powers that were governing the community."* As I was consciously feeling my body re-live this lifetime, the pain increased. The voice spoke to me again and said, *"Breathe deeply."* And I did. *"And Deeper."* Intuitively I knew if I kept the breath going, my body would not take on survival or fear mode, but one of healing. The story and pictures were complete.

   My mind then asked my body what to do next. The response was: "Forgive yourself." And the mind quickly says, "For what?" "Take responsibility for creating this lifetime to have such pain and suffering because of your beliefs." I obey and more visions come. I now see that my beliefs were so strong I acted in a way that offended many, and they questioned the validity of my intuitions.

This I realize is not new to me, as I have experienced this pattern in the very body I am healing now. Curious, I follow with more questions, with complete knowing that I will be freed of this pain by staying with it and going all the way—to healing. My ankle and shoulder pain are subsiding, with each question clarifying a truth within the story. I forgave myself for being so opinionated and forceful that others were offended and for causing my life to end at that time. I then received an inspiration! My God mind offers, *"What if you choose differently now? How might you have lived that life in a more responsible, peaceful way?"*

First there was a struggle to see this situation differently. To not blame other people for the way it was and to not feel victimized by them and the situation. I once again, "forgave myself" for those feelings. I was inspired to create a new scenario where I was more compassionate and understanding, a scenario where I was feeling love towards the people in my community who did not understand my intuitions and in fact disparaged them. The pain in my ankle and shoulder completely released. I was relieved this was over, and my body felt peaceful.

In the next moment, with my eyes still closed, I saw a flash of light so bright I was frightened by it. Calming my mind again to a place of non-worry, I was able to accept that what was happening was my body's natural healing on a cellular, deep, and intense level. The energy I felt was powerful, fast, and filled with love.

Asking my inner knowing about this, the answer came, *"Christ's love and healing—be still, watch, observe and feel."*

I'll do my best to describe this feeling: It came as a very strong yet shimmering heavenly light, like a bolt of lightening strong and direct, and an intense feeling of peace, love and connectedness accompanied it. The energy was so strong I could feel it rejuvenating my body—removing layers of damaged tissue, scar tissue, old cellular patterns, and re-creating past situations and carving out a new way to be NOW.

After seeing and experiencing this intense healing, I realized that my body is so stunningly magnificent. What a gift I have in this body. This is MY body, my magnificent home for me to work out this life's evolution. Its value to my life is truly as my temple, a place for me to reside, heal, and carry out the true purpose for my life. The gratitude from my heart beams as I open up to myself, with love and honor of every cell, atom, molecule, tissue, muscle, ligament, tendon, bone, blood (red and white cells), and every organ in my body. I offer my body genuine heartfelt love and gratitude for being MY body, for being willing to heal, for showing me images that offer me a chance to be a better person in this life. And, I ask forgiveness from my body for all the years of neglect and abuse I have done to it. I thank my angels and God. Slumber comes as I reach completion and I feel each of my cells transform— energetically bathed in Christ's love and golden healing light.

~~NOTES~~

Chapter 6

Sub-Conscious to Conscious

Every Word is a Prayer

I have had puzzling, conflicting questions my whole life. In this healing space these questions are presenting themselves to be answered. For years when I would go to bed, just as I closed my eyes, I would see an unfamiliar face that would come into focus then fade out only to have another face to come into view. There would be a group of ten to fifteen of these faces coming into focus then fading, allowing the next face to appear.

My sense was that these faces were ancient ones asking for my attention. They appeared to be from different eras, possibly different lifetimes of mine, wearing shrouds, old style hats, having beards with long hair, some were bald, some women, some men, and some children. There was one thing in common in all these faces. They looked at me directly into my essence, with a somewhat somber yet inviting gaze. They came to me as I closed my eyes to sleep, beckoning me to pay attention to what they were bringing, but for years I stayed asleep to their pleas. In this healing space as I dreamt, I remembered agreeing to come here to learn and teach others. Now I am being taught by beings in other dimensional realms, and my body is the teaching tool of this physical realm.

The noted doctors and masters, who have ascended—they left their physical bodies—and yearn to teach their mastery and forms of healing to people living on this earth, were my teachers. Albert Einstein and Edgar Cayce, were just two of the more notable ones, while others remained unnamed yet very powerful energies. Some were the spiritual teachers: Christ, Buddha, Mother Mary, and Quan Yin, as well as many Archangels such as Michael, Gabriel, and Raphael. My life path has been to learn trust, and I needed the assistance of each of these teachers. Each experience led me to understand myself in a different way, from a different viewpoint. I learned to ask my body questions instead of my mind and then to listen for the answers instead of already thinking I know the answers. I learned to progressively follow the path my body was leading me down to discover the inner Truths that were revealed through my cellular memory. These are the Truths that my body and soul are here to learn.

I discovered information from my past lives that had an impact on my present life. I remembered lifetimes that I mastered the teachings of the ancient mysteries and, through grace, brought these teachings into my present life (teachings that I was aware of in this lifetime yet wondered how I knew that information). Trusting that intuitive sense of knowing inside me seemed new. It was as if I no longer needed another's approval of me. I approved of me. I trusted myself, and my inner feelings. These feelings became my Truth. The more I spoke my Truth with kindness and love, the more I became aware, I, was speaking a higher Truth.

As I started getting out more, I answered the questions of my friends who wanted to know how I had been healed so fast. In my answers from the truth of my heart in that moment, each person began to say to me that I was quoting books and teachers that I had never read or only glanced at. According to my friends, I was quoting the Bhagavad Gita, St. Francis of Assisi, the Bible, Jesus, teachings from The Ancient Mystery Schools, and the white brotherhood. I was amazed when I heard these responses. I was just feeling inside my body, and sharing what I had learned. The energy of my outer reality must have been felt by these people to mirror my inner reality.

When I went to bed I wasn't sure what I would experience next. What will I be shown? Who was talking to me? My mind wandered with so many questions causing me to feel exhausted by my own thoughts. So, I came up with a clever way to outwit my mind's queries. I promised my mind that when it gets too busy thinking, I would ask it to observe what happens, instead of trying to constantly question, criticize or analyze. As I suggested this to my mind, I instantly felt elated, and relieved—somewhat like I was watching my own life from above me. There was a peaceful sensation, and I was able to allow the healing to continue without my mind becoming a slave to the questions and desperately "wanting" to know the answers.

This process proved to assist me again and again, as often during my sleep I was awakened by jolts of light of many colors and strong yet gentle energy running through my body, or voices speaking to me. Instead of questions or concerns, I watched, and within minutes I had learned from the energy. I felt the energy gracefully healing something in me and then silence, peace. The mind and body were safe. I recognized the mind's activity blocks the flow of healing energy. But when the mind is at peace, the body's natural flow creates healing. When I was at peace with this process, I was learning about healing. I would easily do as I was being guided, and I watched the astounding results. Each morning upon waking, my body experienced easier movement from the healing I had received during the night.

Some nights I would be inspired to use some of the knowledge I gained in reading books like Shakti Gawain's *Creative Visualization*. I love my active imagination, so this was an opportunity to use the energy in a new, creative way. I remembered reading in Dr. Bernie Segal's, *Love, Medicine and Miracles*, that groups he taught to visualize their recovery healed faster after surgery.

When I put these two concepts together, I visualized seeing myself at my most energetic, vital, and happiest. I chose myself as an eight-year-old child who loved to play outside, and was full-of-life. I saw myself in my room making a lager (an instrument to use for playing hopscotch), then going outside and drawing a hopscotch design on the sidewalk in front of my house with my favorite color of chalk. Once the drawing was done I invited my friends over to play with me. I felt every hop in my muscles and legs. I felt my leg muscles stretch and my back bend as I reached down to pick up my lager. I remembered every scent in my neighbors' gardens as I played after dinner that summer. Next, I imagined myself riding my bicycle on the weekends as a twelve year old, and taking myself to the closest mall to shop for little girl things like hair and nail accessories. Afterwards I would stop to have a tasty grilled cheese sandwich and vanilla malt that I loved so much, before the long bike ride home, and then feeling the wind sweeping the hair off my face.

Another healing memory I visualized was when I was in my early 40's, I learned to play tennis and remembered feeling every muscle while working on my serve, with my right arm! That exercise evoked a feeling of fun within me. I had a good serve and the sensation of my muscles and tendons in my arm moving to serve a tennis ball to a willing partner was exciting. Another vision was remembering what a good bowler I used to be and seeing myself in perfect form, smelling the chalk on my hands with the ball up to my nose, ready to make each step moving toward the line and releasing the ball, then the ball hitting all the pins for a strike. Before I fell asleep, using all of my senses, each detail of these scenes would continue in my dreams and my body throughout the night. When I awoke in the morning, there was a tangible change in my energy that translated into body movement becoming easier. After the healing journey with my ankle and right arm, I actually lifted my arm above my head and relearned how to use it. From the time I came home from the hospital I had been learning to use my left hand and arm for writing, brushing my teeth, eating, and other tasks. This morning I slowly and mindfully began to use my right arm again.

As my friends came over to visit or assist me, without filtering my thoughts through my mind, I began asking if they were "in" their bodies. I was seeing something different about them. They would check inside themselves, each time I asked the question. Usually the answer came back, "No." I began to pay close attention to the energy I was feeling, and seeing, as well as the answers my friends gave me, so I could learn something. What did this mean to me, and how would it affect my life? What did it mean to be fully inside your body, or not? It seemed that something pivotal in my understanding was changing.

I learned that my breath kept me inside my body. When I breathed, I was connected to all of me. When I held my breath, stopped on exhale, or paused before bringing in the next breath, it was a chance to disconnect from my body. I realized by asking my friends and remembering in my own life, that I learned to leave my body when I was a young girl. Whenever I was afraid of something I would disconnect, thereby seemingly avoiding all pain in my body. It became a safety mechanism that I used to "save me" when times were tough while growing up. *When I disconnected, the fear became locked in my body*. As I moved through life, when circumstances threatened, fear built in the body and over time, converted into large energetic blocks. Energetic blocks can lead to illness and/or disease, if left unchecked.

After looking closely at myself, it appeared that my first, second and third chakras (the body's energy centers; see glossary) were closed down. These energy centers are connected to: survival (1st chakra); sexuality/creativity (2nd chakra); and personal power and will (3rd chakra). Learning to know myself, and being inside my body is what I came here to experience. Because my childhood had some less than positive experiences, I had "saved" myself by "closing down" my lower chakras and began functioning only out of my higher chakras: heart (4th chakra); throat (5th chakra); third eye (6th chakra); and crown, (7th chakra). All of these chakras are where I connect with my higher, or Spirit self and feel safe.

I lived and functioned out of my higher chakras only, but I paid a high price—my health. I have actually drawn trauma to myself in these lower three chakras because of this disconnection to my body. Many of us have suffered trauma in the lower three chakra areas such as sexual molestation and abuse. When we feel fear, we resist and suppress it within the body in the first three chakras. Somehow we learn to survive out of the upper four chakras, through Spirit. This however is how our bodies get so damaged and suffer illness.

We unconsciously protect ourselves from fear and pain by closing off the lower three chakras and when this happens we stop breathing. When we begin to consciously breathe inside our bodies, and reclaim our responsibility for our health, our first three chakras will open and heal. The pain will diminish and forgiveness can take place. Then love reigns, and your body begins to know you are supporting it with your higher self-love and you are living out the real commitment you are here to experience, which is love. Your body can then be healthy, and you are fulfilling the many reasons why you are here: to heal and to forgive; to love and be loved; to evolve your soul.

Sometime later I had an experience that would prove my reasoning. The year after my fall I appeared to be doing great. I was teaching self-healing classes, traveling, making new friends, writing this book, and experiencing a new level of comfort with the constant unknown. I did not realize how fast paced my life had become. I had allowed myself little to no down time or integration time in quite a while. One day after a ceremony at my home, my Vedic (philosophy and astrology) teacher was giving me an updated reading. He told me something that I interpreted as more difficulties coming. I became fearful and began to cry. Immediately afterwards, someone came to my door and gave me more bad news. It was an instant manifestation of being pushed over an edge while feeling fearful, exhausted, vulnerable, and un-centered. I calmed down, slowed down, and took time to breathe. Everything came into perspective.

Later that evening, I had an experience at a women's circle of sharing. I was asked to begin the sharing. I felt unsettled, and declined to share at that time and passed my turn for later. As I listened to the others I saw a vision of all of us in circle hundreds of years ago and heard my own at that time saying, "I am afraid of every woman in this room (circle)." At that now moment, I realized I had experienced this thought many times previously, in this life, whenever I was in a circle of women, but had resisted having the associated feeling of fear. In that moment I was present to the feeling that was lodged in, old and painful. Now, in this circle, I had stopped breathing and disconnected from my body, re-experiencing these past unconscious memories. I then consciously brought myself into the now moment, cleared old thoughts, and the old resistant energy released.

At about that same moment, the woman sitting next to me touched my back quite spontaneously, and I began feeling myself re-enter my body! I had not even realized until that moment, that I had been out-of-my-body from the time earlier that evening when I interpreted my teacher's reading. This experience shows how subtle the energies are. Once fully back in my body, I saw very clearly that when I am out of my body I am vulnerable to negative situations, past situations and that staying out of my body can generate an unconstructive energy that actually replays old patterns. Once I felt grounded again in my body with my friend's hand on my back and my whole self had re-entered my body, I was able to easily be present and acknowledge how much I loved each woman in the circle. I was again able to be in touch with present feelings of My Self. We were all amazed when I finally shared this realization with the group.

The third week home from the hospital, I was left alone for the first time. With joy I learned all over again how to dress and shower. Now, I appreciate the ability to do these seemingly "small' things." I realized that I would have to "think/plan" out my day now that I was on my own. Just getting out of bed was an interesting experience. I laughed a lot watching myself take each movement into planning. I asked each part of my body to move slowly and carefully so that it would be in sync and also safe. It took me three times longer to get out of bed, move to the bathroom, brush my teeth, and so on. I started the learning process all over again. I was acquiring patience and then gratitude, as small accomplishments turned into larger victories.

By very consciously observing myself in this way, I learned that my thinking was almost completely reactionary. I noticed my reactionary thoughts were mostly about being afraid to move too quickly or incorrectly, because I was constantly mindful that I might hurt or re-injure myself. Rather than go in that direction, I began to use conscious discipline with my mind to tell my body where and how to move in a positive and loving way. My body was feeling empowered, and was being nurtured by me—trusted, by me. Speaking consciously to myself would place another dimension on being in the present moment and creating myself well. The results were amazing. I was improving, sometimes within hours. Sometimes it only took one week to heal what the doctors were telling me would take six weeks.

When my friend Diane took me to see Dr. Bonatus 10 days after the fall, (remember when I was in the hospital I said I would be out of that cast in one week?),

50 Feet in 4 Seconds

I walked in on crutches and held onto the counter as the nurses asked me questions. I began telling them about my healing, and soon I saw heads turning in the room around me. I could feel everyone listening to my story as if there was a crowd around me listening to every word, including the patients in the waiting room close by.

I was escorted to the exam room where I waited for the doctor. A nurse came in and asked me if I was ready to have the soft cast on my right arm removed. I happily agreed. I had about 20 staples from mid-forearm to about 3 inches above my elbow. As she was taking the cast off my arm, she asked if I wanted Novocain to deaden the area around the staples. As I began answering her "No", she interrupted me saying"

"I've never seen the staples popping out of anyone's wound before!"

"What?" I said. "What are you talking about?"

She said, "Look," and pointed to my arm.

I twisted my body around and was shocked to see the staples were already out of the wound ¼ of an inch! She said, "This will hurt a bit," and I'm thinking, "Not at all," while she removed the staples one by one. I could not feel a thing! And remember, without Novocain. She kept looking at me watching for some reaction; there was none. When Dr. Bonatus came into the room to check my arm he was also a bit surprised, then jokingly asked me if I was ready to have the cast off my left leg. I answered a confident and excited, "Yes."

Sub-Conscious to Conscious

Each day, for ten days prior to the doctor's visit, I had been doing isometric muscle toning exercises within the muscles of my left leg. On about the fourth day I felt the swelling diminish, and my leg and ankle muscles becoming stronger. Dr. Bonatus removed the cast and I left the office that day on my own two feet, without crutches. Everyone watched me walk out of the office, as I heard the whispers around me, "She just fell off a 50-foot cliff 10 days ago!"

During my fourth week of healing I felt it would be helpful to be in the warm healing salt water of the ocean. I love floating my body in the ocean. My friend offered to escort me to Puerto Penasco, Mexico, the closest ocean available.

The day before we left, I met with my friend Miriam, who was upset about a recent relationship problem. I heard the voice inside me say, *"Lend her your essential oil blend called 'Joy'."* What I said to her was, "I will let you borrow my Joy." In that moment I felt a shift in my energy, as if by handing her the bottle, I in fact, gave her my joy.

About two hours later I became irritated and upset for no apparent reason. This did not fit with where I had been for four weeks, so I tuned inside my body to ask what was happening. I patiently awaited my answer, which did not come until I returned home from Mexico.

Four days later Miriam returned my bottle of the essential oil blend "Joy" to me, and I immediately felt the peaceful warm energy healing return. It was as if the energy was connected to the bottle. I then remembered what I had said to her when I loaned it to her. My language spoke my joy leaving me, and returning when she gave it back. This was a very powerful example of words in action. Remember to be mindful of what you say. Your words become your reality.

As Ghandi taught:
Keep your thoughts positive because your thoughts become your words
Keep your words positive because your words become your behavior
Keep your behavior positive because your behavior become your habits
Keep your habits positive because your habits become your values
Keep your values positive because your values become your destiny

Bliss is the closest word to describe how I was feeling. And, I made it a personal quest to attain that state again, consciously and permanently. The question then became how? I was learning about the human "process." I was learning that humans "are" a "process." As we learn, we integrate what we have learned and then learn more. This is accomplished one step at a time, one moment at a time, based on what we are committed to and what our priorities are.

After diligent practice for four weeks, paying conscious attention to my body, I was healed. I could tell by my agility, and freedom of movement. I was interested in starting yoga on my living room floor, and I did. Very slowly at first, each day breathing deeply into each muscle group while stretching and talking very gently to my body. I thanked my body and praised it for all the wonderful healing it had done and that I would honor it by keeping conscious choice in my life. I was committed and promised my body that I would practice every day the processes I had learned that helped me heal. I promised I would do this as long as I lived. I realized then, there was no other reason for me to live than to be the best I could be, by honoring these practices and living my life as an experiment. I wondered how my life would change being dedicated to this new practice as a way of life?

By being given the grace to live through an experience such as this, to honor what I learned which made my healing so unique, (I had never heard of anyone healing like this before), seemed an awesome path. I continued this way of thinking, breathing, and choosing for my highest good in every situation, rather than using the past or reacting as I had done before. I felt liberated! Freedom, on every level of my being—freedom to be in the moment, choosing clearly and consciously. What a different way to be in life than ever before! No one can give you freedom. It is a state of mind and body that you achieve. The "knowing" that is inside the body, is more Truth than we can ever learn by studying books.

It is a miracle to realize this, and to be able to pass it on. It is even more of a miracle to live it! I pieced together, over three years of deep meditation, what happened night after night during those four weeks and all of my life prior to this experience, to achieve more clarity so I could stay in this co-creation with my life.

As my friends continued to visit and help me do daily chores, they would marvel at my improvement. They were more convinced than ever of their designation, "Miracle Woman." We connected with each other almost without words, instead through our hearts. Their eyes would tell the story of their love, desire and eagerness for my new awareness to be heard and witnessed.

Whether I was at home visiting with friends telling intricate details of this powerful healing story, or meeting friends whom I hadn't spoken to since the fall, I answered humbly, honestly and in the moment, each time I was asked, "How did you heal so quickly?" People I did not even know seemed destined to connect with me by eye contact, stare for a few moments and then ask me if I was the one they had heard about. They all wanted to know how I did it. All I said was "I surrendered."

I noticed wherever I went people connect with me through my eyes: strangers, children, and the elderly—as if they know me or recognize me. When asked, I share the story of how I healed so quickly with as many people as are interested. Each time it is as if I were telling it for the first time.

Even today when I teach a class or when talking to someone who is interested in how I learned to self-heal, I tell the story as if my memory comes from the present moment and am telling it for the first time. Many times recounting the story I learn new insightful details that can help the person I am in conversation with, or me myself. I began to be curious about why people wanted to ask about my healing. It was so strange for people to be so curious about me, so I asked God what to do.

Patience again, after a year of asking this question the answer I received in crystal clear clarity was, "Teach them."

I was ready to meditate again. My muscles were not stretched enough to sit in lotus position, so I walked into my meditation room and stood in front of my altar. I expressed much gratitude for being alive, and for those blessed beings who assisted in my healing. In a moment, I found myself deeply in meditation. I had my eyes open, which was a new way for me to meditate.

A feeling of deep confidence and knowing was coming over me. A moment later I felt a very strong energy around me, then within me. As I looked around the room I felt my hands pulsating with golden light streaming from my fingertips, and then looking down at my feet. I saw the ends of a white robe, while standing on sand with open-toed sandals, and smelled a musty scent in the air. I felt the energy of Christ very strong within my body. I was beaming, the most beautiful feeling of pure love and golden light exuding from my body. I felt blessed, grateful, and awed all at the same time.

On the fifth week I began aerobics again. I had been taking classes for a while, before I fell. My muscle memory returned easily and I got into pretty good shape within a few weeks. I remember one day walking to my car after a few months of class, and I felt my hips loose enough to wiggle. I was delighted to get my wiggle back!

I was continuously living in a very high state of bliss. It was a different state of being than I had ever experienced before. I realized I had no judgments of anyone or anything—that if my mind had a thought that was negative, it would vanish of its own accord.

When my friends would come over to give me treatments such as Reiki, Traegar, lymphatic massage, or subtle body energy work, they would tell me they were being healed in my energy.

From that point on, I began the discovery of how, why, and what difference it made to have bliss in my life. I have found that through this experience I have gained perspective, love, and being the best I can be as my reality. So a "quest-i-on" really becomes a *quest I am on*, in its truest form. All the concepts I had learned from books, workshops and teachers had arrived in my life as "experience." At that point, the vision I saw in March 1997 turned into the written word—this book. It was, "We have a job to do here, much bigger than what we have been doing. The time is NOW. Do it NOW. Do that thing you love, NOW. We have been waiting for things to be "perfect," or for "some day." Some day never comes. The time is NOW."

What was presented to me while healing was a series of steps—a relearning and shedding of my old personality, ego, and perceptions of knowing how the world was to me. These steps and discoveries were so exciting to me. I felt the enthusiasm well up inside of me to teach others and accomplish this ongoing attainment of bliss in a world with many perceptions, many choices, and many ways of living.

~~NOTES~~

Chapter 7

Asking for Grace in Final Surgery

Honor the completions in life, then, begin anew.

Four and one-half months had gone by since I had seen Dr. Bonatus for my routine checkup. I had not seen him because of some odd circumstances, which kept me away. In June, I neglected to write down the appointment date in my calendar. So, I was thinking and trying to remember when my appointment date was. Then one day, quite by intuition, I called the doctor's office to find out when the appointment was and to reschedule, because I thought I probably had missed it. The person answering on the other end proclaimed I had just missed it by an hour!

In July, I went to Flagstaff for my appointment and was asked to leave because my insurance carrier had not given me a referral to the Surgeon's office. I was told the doctor would not see me unless I could pay for the appointment. On this day I felt like a rejected child. I did not argue with them about their position, because it was obviously their policy.

They claimed everyone in the office told me prior to my appointment that I had to have this referral in order for the doctor to see me. It was so bizarre that I felt like I was back in school and could say nothing. I was being told that I could not have what I wanted, just like a child in fourth grade. So, I reluctantly left the office,

Asking for Grace in Final Surgery

and the rest of the day I felt that same bizarre, heavy energy of the past.

Then I had an epiphany! I suddenly realized that two very difficult emotions I have been plagued with most of my life were rejection and abandonment. They came up in my life now, to heal and relive in a conscious way. I had a secret that I had been withholding from my immediate family. I was terrified that they would never forgive me for not telling them.

Unconsciously, I had re-created that same reaction and feelings in my outer world—fear of being rejected and abandoned that I thought I would get from my family. Life is a great healer. Once we see it that way and accept it, we can bless everything that happens to us and with a confidence and knowing, proclaim, "This is for my healing."

When I finally got to see Dr. Bonatus in September for my appointment, he said, "I see here in your chart you are interested in taking the hardware out of your arm." I said, "Yes." Previously, everyone told me never to expect being able to take the metal and screws out. And if by some miracle, they did take them out, it could only be after a year's time. Each time I heard that answer from someone, I heard in my body the response, "September" and detached the energy of knowing to allow the natural flow.

Dr. Botanus said, "We can do that, let's see the x-rays." As he put the x-rays up on the light board I saw two screws floating around outside of the metal plate, in four and one-half months! I was amazed. My body all along had told me when it was healed, and this was

50 Feet in 4 Seconds

further proof. As he thoughtfully pondered over the x-rays he said, "You are healed!" I said, "I know." He then said, "When would you like to schedule the surgery?" I said "Right away." It was mid-September when he gave me this news and the surgery was for Friday, October 10th. (It was fitting that it was Yom Kippur, around the beginning of the Jewish New Year and the day of fasting. My mother would have loved the synchronicity as much as I did).

I had some time to think about how having choice in the present moment would effect my surgery. I planned every detail, as if I had complete control of having all my wishes fulfilled from pre-op to post-op. I watched my design come to pass exactly as I had planned it.

When I went in for pre-op the week before the surgery, I interviewed with the doctor's assistant. I mentioned to her that I was interested in having only a local anesthetic rather than a full body anesthesia and that I would prefer to have the homeopathic remedy Arnica, which helps the body manage pain and assists with healing. The nurse said we would have to talk to the doctor.

In about 15 minutes Dr. Bonatus was standing there in front of us. I asked him as I had asked her, and he agreed to all of my requests. Before I could say anything to the nurse again, she said to me timidly, "If you like, you can bring some aromatherapy like lavender or peppermint to breathe while you are in surgery." My eyes lit up. I said, "Yes my favorite is lavender and ylang ylang." Then I asked if I could bring my favorite music. She approved this, then

Asking for Grace in Final Surgery

followed with an offering to balance my chakras energetically, prior to surgery. I was so excited to receive all these wonderful supportive gifts from the medical establishment.

I asked her, "How did you learn about energy, are you trained in Reiki?"

She said "No, I learned it at the Holistic Nurses Association."

Wow, I had no idea there was such an association! Thank God! Then the topper—as she took out her date book and marked her calendar she said,

"I will come in Thursday night, the night before your surgery, and sage the operating and recovery room."

I told her I was so happy to hear this, and very grateful. I would have asked for that also but thought it too presumptuous. I also asked if I could have each member of the original surgery team because I wanted this surgery to be the last one I would ever have.

I shared with the nurse and my doctor that I had already planned to have a ceremony at my house with my friends. I told her it would include giving the entire team all of the assistance they desired to perform their highest functions on me, and everyone they were scheduled to operate on that day. They both smiled and gave me a hearty, warm "Thank you," that exuded appreciation.

God gives all that we ask for and more, when we are clear and unattached, we can receive it all.

~~NOTES~~

Chapter 8

Ceremony on the Mountain

"Difficult and painful as it is we must walk on in the days ahead with an audacious faith in the future. When our days become dreary with low-hovering clouds of despair, and when our nights become darker than a thousand midnights, let us remember that there is a creative force in this universe, working to pull down the gigantic mountains of evil, a power that is able to make a way out of no way and transform dark yesterdays into bright tomorrows. Let us realize the arc of the moral universe is long, but it bends toward justice."

Dr. Martin Luther King, Jr.

Around the seventh week of my recovery I received very strong guidance to climb up that same mesa again.

"There will be eight people with you, bring sacred objects, and do a ceremony to clear any fear on the land left from your fall, and restore light on that spot."

I was exercising my body every other day at this point and feeling strong, yet still moving very carefully. I had learned to follow the voice I had come to trust, but there remained some concern about hiking up that hill so soon. I kept that communication in my heart until the weekly potluck when I shared my message with my spiritual family. By the end of the evening, I had a group of men and women, my sisters and brothers, volunteer to join me on Saturday, exactly seven weeks after the fall.

That Saturday morning I gathered the sacred objects, the necklace I was wearing when I fell, a handful of fresh flowers, and some sage. I realized everything I gathered were all gifts to me, and I was about to make them gifts to the land. The necklace was especially dear to me. It was a gift from a dear friend from the late 80's. She made me a six-pointed star from an old ring of hers, and added a Herkimer diamond crystal in the center. It was one of my treasures. But now for me, there is no such thing as a treasure. I have my life and God; everything else is a bonus.

   When I met my spiritual family at the trailhead, there were four sisters and four brothers, just as I had been told. Each brought something to either give to the land, or be used in the ceremony for the land.

   As we walked up the hill, each one had special attention focused on me, and how I was coping with the terrain. For most of the hike, my brothers flanked each side of me, and at the steepest point of the hill whoever was in front offered his belt loops for me to hold on to, pulling me slowly up the hill.

   About 30 yards before we reached the mouth of the cave, I had to stop. I was really pushing myself, and this was as far as I felt I could go. I asked everyone if we could do the ceremony there and they all agreed.

   As I looked around to find a flat rock to sit on and rest, I noticed there were some dark spots on several rocks below my feet. I sat and looked closer at the spot I was resting on, then looked up and around at the cave, then back down at the spots on the rocks. I realized those spots were dried drops of my blood! I was sitting directly on the spot that I landed on when I fell. It was the perfect place to have the ceremony, just as I had been told.

A few of my brothers and one sister wanted to make the climb through the cave to really feel what it must have felt like for me. They went all the way up to the mesa, and on the way down stopped on the ledge and looked at where I was now sitting. They could barely fathom what it must have been like that day exactly seven weeks before.

After their hike, each one of them came up to me individually and shared their love and compassion for what I had experienced. We then sang, chanted, played drums, and lit the sage. We prayed to Great Spirit to allow this area to be cleansed of any fear and that each person who would walk through this sacred land would be honored and in joy for each step of discovery each of them made for themselves. I had my eyes closed and felt very deeply the experience I had been allowed to live through. While my eyes were closed, I saw a picture of myself lying on these rocks and then rising up, wiping off the dirt from my backside and happily walking down the mountain to my future.

There was a little girl who remembered who she is
and who she was
Now she has grown,
matured, and she lives for others by divine blessings:
ease, grace, joy, and choice.

~~NOTES~~

Chapter 9

Receiving Grace in Final Surgery

Love comes in many forms."- God

The following week I went in for surgery. This was an out-patient surgery and I was fifth in line for that day. I patiently waited my turn while Dr. Bonatus operated on every patient that day. Just as the nurses were readying me to go in the room, Dr. Lee my Anesthesiologist came to my bedside. I was told he was still out of town on vacation and could not be there. He told me he had come home from vacation a bit early because he heard I asked for him.

Delighted to see him and to receive my wish of completion, I asked him if I could have a local anesthetic, because I wanted to stay awake during the surgery. He told me he did not recommend it but he would honor my request, and if I felt any pain he would be there to add more anesthetic if necessary.

It was an interesting experience for me. I had no concerns whatsoever about pain, since I knew my body more intimately than ever before at this point. Being completely conscious during the surgery seemed the optimum choice.

During the surgery I felt Dr. Bonatus opening my scar and removing each screw and then finally the plate with a bit of pulling and tugging because some scar tissue had grown over the metal. Then he scraped my elbow of scar tissue because I could not straighten my arm all the way. I felt the joy of having my arm be perfect and new after much trauma. As the doctors made small talk during surgery, I remember boldly offering them "coaching" on whatever it was they were talking about.

It was quite an experience and went even better than planned, which was with ease, grace, and joy. My body had asked me to fast from food even beyond the normal period Dr. Bonatus asked of me, from 8 pm the night before surgery. My body's instructions were to clear out all the toxicity in my body. That included drugs from all prior surgeries, my thyroid surgery and radioactive treatment in 1976, all the antibiotics and pain relievers I had ever taken since childhood, and all the x-rays I had received.

The fast would last as long as it needed, and I would know when it was complete by clear urination. It happened exactly that way on the third day after surgery. I had followed instructions well, and my body was very happily healed.

After removing the metal from my arm the swelling went down in one week, as I claimed it would. This was another lesson in stating clearly and specifically what I choose for my life.

When I checked in with the doctor a week later, he gave me the green light to exercise all I wanted, and move my arm in all directions. Dr. Bonatus and I built a nice rapport between us that I felt very deeply. I am so grateful to him for his genuine openness and his willingness to let me experiment with what I felt was

Receiving Grace in Final Surgery

"right" for me, and not to impose his views. I am especially grateful for his honoring my wishes in a non-judgmental way, and allowing me the right to make choices based on my inner guidance as this process revealed itself to me.

    Twenty days later I'm getting bodywork done on my arm and shoulder, and it feels as though the programming of a new body I have asked for has arrived. My right arm is responding like my left one, and is completing the healing at rapid rates, increasing in strength, rotation, flexion, and extension. The shoulder is loosening up as well, and the little bit of pinching in my right upper arm is getting better every day.

~~NOTES~~

Chapter 10

<u>Learning to Unlearn</u>

Your judgments are all that separate you from God

For about six years prior to my fall, my mantra was, "I will, to will, thy will", from "A Course in Miracles", a self-study course I did for three years. This mantra sounded like a good idea and felt good in my body to allow God to enter my life and show me why I am here.

I had no idea that the "will" part of that mantra would mean the death of my ego. When I fell off that cliff, every part of my life as I had known it—changed. My brain literally shut down what I had known, and made available more cells to receive the grace of God. I began to see things—energy—around people, buildings, and inanimate objects. Nature became my best friend.

I began communicating with animals, like nothing you have seen in animated movies. They would actually tell me what was in their heart, their purpose. They told me what they really needed, not what people wanted to give them. And they taught me, by answering my deepest internal questions. They also gave me guidance as from God.

A good example is the first time I went to see Ammachi (or Amma as she is called by her devotees), the "Hugging Saint" from India who has several Ashrams in the western states. About a year after my fall I received my first hug from her, after hours of waiting in line. She communicated telepathically with me while I meditated moving up the line to receive my hug, telling me how blessed I was. While in her motherly compassionate arms I completely merged into her body, and had no definition of her or me. That hug was too luscious to stand up and immediately return to my seat. I chose to be near her energy for a while so I sat near her on the stage in humble prayer for a few moments to deepen the energy I was feeling.

Strangely no one asked me to leave the stage. Then, as if to awaken me from a trance-like state, I noticed a fly buzzing around me.

I gently pointed my fore-finger which became a perch for it to land upon. I stared at this fly for a while, finally asking what it wanted. Its eyes turned directly toward mine and telepathically it said to me, "I came to see you."

I responded, "Is there something you would you like me to know?"

The fly responded mindfully, waiting for my readiness to learn. "I came here to answer your question."

I felt honored, yet wondered what my question was. My focus and attention dropped into my heart and the question popped up, "When will I be directed on what I am to do next?" The fly began traveling up and down my fingers, going from one finger to the next, doing the same thing over and over again. When it came to my pointer finger once again, it stopped and looked at me to see if I had gotten the answer. I was in deep contemplation and gratitude for my hug and from seeing Amma, (as she is called by her devotees) for the first time. I couldn't grasp with my mind what the fly's response to my question was, so I went even deeper into my being for the answer.

What came to me was that I had been going along my path for many years, though not believing in what I was doing. I would change directions, and go along again and again, still not believing or trusting. I suddenly realized that this time, there was no reason to turn away from this path. I had chosen, and was blessed with the grace of truth and knowledge. Now I could fully trust this would be my path for the rest of my life. Although it might take many forms, being a messenger for God in a practical way for people would be my life's work. As my heart opened wider and a smile crept upon my lips, I thanked the fly and it flew away, then I bowed to Amma again, knowing that every being has consciousness and, not one thing is ever a mistake.

My personal life changed so much. I stopped watching TV or news programs. The energy felt very disruptive to my state of bliss because of the lies I felt we all were being told. I felt there was so much stretching of the truth that it hurt my gut. That is where I now know my truth center to be, the center of my being, my intuition, my connection with God.

For the first three years after the fall, I spent most of my time in silence: either in meditation and communion with the delicious energy of God, or as an observer watching my friends interact with each other.

All the while, I was observing my own mind as I practiced being in silence, letting go of my thoughts, and being in the moment.

Since my fall, I realized that one moment in time changed my entire life. My daily practice was and still is made up of the many teachings that God gave me. Each practice given for a day, a week, a month, a year, or even for several years depending upon my own need to learn the particular practice. I knew when the practice was complete, because it became natural—a natural way of seeing, feeling, or being in my everyday life. This is my path: to practice thinking God mind and speaking God word all day every day, to become my natural state of being.

I believe, as I share with you in this book or in the seminars and classes I teach, that practices like this will help humanity move into a higher state of consciousness. We will easily be able to let go of past anger, hurt, and violent activities upon ourselves individually, and each other collectively as a whole. I have found that this practice has changed every part of my life. This includes: my relationships, my businesses, love for myself, for animals, nature, and people. It has changed my thinking, my feelings and every part of me—rearranged to a state of higher consciousness.

Even as I wrote this book, I would start writing only after I "cleaned up," and readied myself to meet my God-self. Then I would meditate and light a candle, chanting silently "Om Namah Shivaya." (See glossary) As I wrote each paragraph I closed my eyes before the words would come for the next paragraph. After all these changes, I now live and practice every part of my life as sacred.

During these years of practice I have learned that I am enough, that I have enough and that I am loved. I have learned I have both little and much, and that neither matters. I have had guidance and assistance from many realms and have learned to honor them and everyone else as myself. This has helped me to speak differently as I interact with people on a daily basis. I am approved of, appreciated, recognized, and respected—all the things I wanted before—I always had them, I just didn't see or know that I had them. Most of all, I know that I am deeply loved in every second of every day no matter what I think of myself at that time. I live each moment as it is, and I have learned to keep my language clear and simple, so that I speak to others as God speaks to me.

Every word is a prayer.

I have overcome my fear of death, and many other illusions that I/We collectively carry in our consciousness, knowing they are only as real as I would have them be. Also, if I interact with anything such as death (an ego based mind made-up concept), I can see the difference consciousness makes in the way I deal with such concepts in my life. Most of all I have learned to live by the Universal Laws and honor them as sacred, applying them to all my activities. I have learned that I am you, and you are me.

~~NOTES~~

Chapter 11

Divine Message

"What will happen when one woman writes the truth about her life. The world will split open."
– *Muriel Rukeyser*

God told me: *we chose to come here in a body*. That body, having a myriad of intricacies, can make our lives wretched with complexities—or we can have our lives simple. How we make them simple is to understand who we truly are. We are God beings in expression living out this life as designed and co-created to carry out our destiny in physical form. Until we do, we do not remember who we are. Everyone has a certain time in their life when the remembering takes place. It is spontaneous, usually unexpected, and at that moment you "know" who you are and why you are here. Everything in your life comes into a grand focus. Many answers to questions that you have been asking during your sleep, dreams, or illusory states all will become clear. You will be One with everything and your mind will cease. *It is what you choose to do next that makes the difference for the human being in your skin.*

God asked me to share with you to live in your body—to honor that your body is your vehicle, your temple—to move in and through your life, experiencing all the good and not so good. We no longer will ascend – we will do that when we die and leave our body. At this time our collective intent is to be carried out in human form, bringing the light of the divine within our precious cells.

Take life as it comes, choose and make wise choices, in the moment. Notice abuse, (inside and outside of you), and take care to be the light and the dark, honoring your true self. Live the diversity. Learn from the balance of opposites. Be honest, responsible, and "know thyself."

Knowing thyself for me, has been a life-long pursuit, and one surely worth continuing. God wishes that we all gift ourselves with "know thyself" as a life long pursuit because we are all worthy, more than we can truly ever know. Grow through your fears. As you have your dark nights of the soul, reclaim your soul into your body. Know that the moment fear comes it is for your growth and bless the assistance you have from all dimensions, your Angels and guides, and the love that is given to you just for being you. When you stay connected in moments like this, you are keeping your presence and attention with God, so grace can take over in each situation and you can experience the liberation offered to you.

It is such a blessing to be here on the earth at this time and to use our precious consciousness to usher in the new millennium. You chose to be here and you are given much assistance, so please ask and trust that it is yours and give much gratitude to your Angels and guides for being here for you.

Please understand that your body is precious and a highly technological wonder built as a temple for God.

Divine Message

When you know and accept who you are, then your body becomes finely tuned to align with your thoughts and actions in this lifetime. Most of your lives have been lived in only a portion of your body. That is, in the upper half of your body, from the heart up. The lower half of your body—known as the base, sexual, and will centers—are where your traumas and pain are stored. These areas have been working only to accomplish one thing: instinctual survival. With the upper half alive, your connection to God can, and does exist as long as you are alive and in your body.

Please do the breathing and meditation exercises in this book daily, to open up, enliven, and give consciousness to the lower half of your body. This will activate more knowing within you. This may even prepare you for a Divine "knowing" or "awakening" to who you truly are. It is this simple. You already are perfect, there is nothing to change. You have done nothing wrong in your life. You haven't yet recognized that all the choices, decisions, and dramas that you have lived through were part of a perfect plan to knowing who you truly are. There are no mistakes, coincidences or accidents. Everything you have done—and haven't done—is perfectly aligned to learn and know who you truly are: a Divine being. Let go of needing anything, and just BE.

Do your dreams. Live your dreams. Know that you can have anything and be everything you have dreamed. Today. Claim it. You claim your right to "have" and "be" who and what you truly desire. You have put off the things your heart has told you for so long—let go and do them now. There is no later, it does not exist. There is only NOW.

Divine Message

~~NOTES~~

Chapter 12

Simple Daily Healing Practices Utilizing Universal Principles

*Day by day as we heal, the world heals
and we all find out how many different forms 'love' comes in*

Many of us have grown up with the belief that we are selfish. Many of us have turned that so called selfishness into guilt. Whether we feel selfish or not, guilt exists in our collective programming and therefore in the cells within our body. Being selfish hides the true you. Being selfish keeps us ill in our beliefs. I have come to realize utilizing Universal principles, that to have a life of selfless service means realizing that as you give you receive, as you cause you see the effect, as you are present to the Now, time releases its hold on you. Being self-full is the word that feels true to me, not self-ish. Being self-full gives my life a new road in which to create the life I'm really choosing as a co-creation with God.

I can give and give and give, but if I become empty from my giving and do not realize it, my energy drains and I leave my body, mind, and spirit vulnerable. When I consciously give to myself as I give to others, my body, mind, and spirit are rejuvenated and I gain more and more energy, rather than less and less. I refill, rejuvenate, and stay present enough to know when giving to others is out of balance for me. I can

Simple Daily Healing Practices Utilizing Universal Principles

receive from others and also give to myself and become self-full, full of love. Stress can no longer exist in this way of being, therefore ultimate health results.

Feel your feelings, speak your truth for who you really are, not a made up version to suit your ego's needs or to fit society's standards. Be yourself and you will know what true freedom is. As you make this claim to your self, your life will naturally change.

Things will come up that you have ignored or neglected, or put off to do tomorrow. Putting off things on your "to do list" until tomorrow, escalates stress in your life. Doing each thing on the list as you can, in the moment, keeps you in the flow of your life.

Little by little you will begin to confront the things that you have not done in a way that has compassion for you. You will hear your repetitive old way of thinking, and a lot of reasons why you cannot, should not, or do not have the time to finish your list. When your mind's thinking comes clearly into consciousness, connected with God, you then have a choice. You can believe what you have been hearing all these years, OR choose another path; a path that empowers you and feels really good in your gut and heart. What feels really good is the path to truth, your truth, and become congruent with who you genuinely are.

Self-healing through your inner God-self will eventually lead you into a fine vibrational frequency in your body. You may experience more sensitivity (please do not protect yourself or your energy), allow it to flow from within. People often say to me "how can I protect myself?" or "how can I get rid of that thought?"

There are many ways you can take care of yourself. You cannot "protect" yourself from anything or "get rid" of anything. Both of those thoughts are coming from fear, and when you are responding from fear you will constantly be in the mindset of fear and what you will be doing is protecting yourself for the rest of your life. When you come from love you are offering yourself a space to clear energies, because other people's energies and fears are none of your concern. Other people's energies and fears are not who you are and my question to you is do you really want to be involved in other people's lives at that level? Don't you already have enough on your own plate to deal with? To experience your love, for yourself, within your body, is the greatest joy you can give yourself.

   We live in a world of duality. For every positive there is a negative. Sometimes this looks like polarity, things opposing each other. When you live (by this I mean where you come from inside your consciousness about you and your life), in the world from the perspective that what happens to you is either "right" or "wrong," you are living duality. This is one of the ways the separation from God source affects us. (See glossary)

   Most of the clients I work with experience this on a daily basis. By acknowledging and being responsible and seeing experiences fitting into either "right" or "wrong," you will continue to see duality in your life. As you use these practices you will see how your consciousness lives "right" or "wrong."

Simple Daily Healing Practices Utilizing Universal Principles

After using the following techniques until they were second-nature, I knew how to access my personal truth within a moment. One of the many simple practices that I gave myself when I realized this is: as I would go through my daily life, was asking myself, "How do I see this?" when something irritated or upset me. Usually the answer would be somewhere in the gamut of "this is right for me" or "this is not right." Then I would take that energy into my heart and breathe into it. After a few minutes something would pop up in my consciousness about why I saw it "right" or "not right." Then I would accept that it is that way—either "right" or "wrong" for me and fully allow myself to have that experience, to think that way, or to be programmed that way, whatever the case may have been. Then it would all melt away and disappear. In offering myself full acceptance, I forgave myself and became self-responsible at the same time. My heart would expand or open up and I felt lighter. Also, my self-responsibility became heightened so I could be aware of how I sabotage myself and then make a new choice.

You may also experience your gifts (multi-dimensional brain) opening up. You may discover that you are more clairvoyant (vision), clairsentient (feeling), or clairaudient (hearing). (See glossary for definitions). You may feel energy moving around within your brain. You may see many colored lights and patterns when your eyes are closed. These are a few of the signs that your brain's structure is changing. Your gifts will be revealed to you in a clear way. This is a time to trust. Be calm, breathe, and allow the changes. You will see how these changes will show up in your life in your daily activities.

Be kind to yourself with your own self-love as you shift, and grace will be with you always. Be responsible to your changes. Talk to and learn from those who have gone before you, who have recognized and are in touch with their own changes. Also, share your changes with those asking for your assistance. Feel the love inside you and experience for yourself what it feels like to be the receiver of the love that you give. When you have thoughts that are unloving towards yourself—stop—take a breath and say what you mean to say, removing the harshness and parenting style words you hear in your head. They are not yours, and you do not have to keep them. Re-create them for who you are NOW. After some practice you will find your beautiful mind a loving support to you and all you choose to do.

Upgrade your thoughts and ideas about your life, goals, and dreams on a regular basis. You will find that if you keep goals, dreams, and ideas from years ago, they may come after you have changed and then they would be unwanted in your new consciousness, I feel it's important to keep current with goals, dreams, and ideas on a regular basis to keep your consciousness current. I will give you an example. Once I had moved from the hectic city life to rural Sedona I began to change but I hadn't changed my goals. Years prior when I lived in the city I had this idea of a job I would love. I wanted to work in a large corporation. The people that hire me would use my training skills to create teams and I would manage a staff of ten. My salary was spelled out exactly

Simple Daily Healing Practices Utilizing Universal Principles

in terms of pay and benefits. When my husband and I moved to Sedona we agreed I would have a job and he would start a business for us. Almost immediately after we made that agreement a neighbor came over to get acquainted and during that conversation my skills were revealed. The next day she made me a fantastic job offer as front desk and reservations manager of a popular hotel. They hired me because of my background in training and transition, with the salary and the specifics I wanted. After two weeks I was ready to quit. I was not getting to do what I was hired for, which was training. My job became to manage people working in an environment of crisis. My workday consisted of 16 grueling hours, six days a week, none of which were the pictures I had when I made this goal. My bosses convinced me to stay but after two months I became a nagging, horrible person and I quit. It took me six months to decompress from this experience. During that decompression time I realized I had made that goal four years before this experience! This situation made me highly aware of how the past becomes the present when we are not conscious.

   Conflicts in the body, mind, and emotions can and do cause illness. When you "know thyself," you know every cell, every atom, every muscle, bone, and ligament, and you are connected to the Divine within. You can heal through your connection. By honoring yourself as human and Divine, you will heal. Be the beautiful Being that you are from the inside out. You will also learn how your mind thinks, your emotions move, react, and respond to outside stimuli, and how your spirit/soul dwells within. You will know how to be with them as one unit, rather than as parts of you, separated, divided, and fearful.

From many years of working with clients I have learned that each person has their perfect path and they are already on that path, although they may not realize it. I have also learned from them that in each situation they face, they champion themselves to be the best they can in that moment. When they do not know who they are, they will usually be very hard on themselves and turn situations into punishment. When they know who they are, they turn situations in their life into blessings, learning experiences, and a full empowerment to move ahead with joy into the teaching they just experienced.

The following techniques were given to me to learn to "know thyself." Please use them daily, and share them generously with others. Practiced every day, each in its own way, they will expand your sense of yourself inside your body, clear energy blockages that can cause eventual pain or disease, and bring you into a centered and grounded space so you can deal with whatever life is presenting you.

~~NOTES~~

Technique #1

Discernment Technique

We have so many choices in our lives today. The stimulation life gives us and our body is tremendous, so we develop discernment. We can healthfully manage a large percentage of the retinal stimulation (stimulation from images through the eyes) that comes to us through people, words, computers, television, huge images on billboards, freeways, and etcetera.

When the healing of my broken bones was complete at the fourth week mark and I began to leave my home to workout again, it was the first time that I had been anywhere other than in my back yard. While wonderful on one level, my body began to feel constricted and tight, especially in my solar plexus (third chakra). Immediately, my God-mind asked my body what happened. I began the wondrous journey of healing on my own without anything to assist me, which I call true Self-Responsibility.

That first response told me that my solar plexus was where the outside energy affected me, and my body. In the past, I made that "feeling" a story that told me I had to close myself down, be more observant, talk less, and keep my feelings to myself, or some other untruth. However, now my body showed me how to take that fear of being my true self around people, and bring love to that area of my body. That gave my mind freedom of expression and my body did not have to protect itself

Technique #1: Discernment Technique

any longer. I immediately learned what a "yes" feeling is and what a "no" feeing is, in my body. A "yes" feeling opens me up and I feel free. When I feel free I am choosing openness and feeling what is right for me at that time and I feel empowered. A "no" feeling constricts me, closes me down. When I feel constricted I will take that as a "no" for me and politely choose again.

I began to practice every day all day when my body felt constricted in any way, I would breathe love into that space to keep it safe, open, and allowing. This practice lasted for years until it became a natural way of being for me, and my ego. I quickly learned that humans are process oriented. When we honor our processes, we can then be conscious of how we are being affected in life. We can then alter any experience that does not serve us (that is past based), choose newly for that moment and move forward, into a space that will serve us in a more loving way. I choose love. You may choose peace, or joy, or gratitude, it really does not matter what your choice is, just choose what feels good inside you. Allow your body to really experience that feeling. Then, come from that feeling in your interactions throughout the day. After some practice with this, you will see how easy it is to empower yourself all day long.

When you allow your mind to become curious about what is happening inside you or with your life, you create a presence of learning to allow the ego to become real and conscious. I believe this is pivotal so you can learn to discern what has been running your life up until now. At any moment you can stop—listen to what you have been and are listening to, and then what is true for you. The ego will love having its voice known. It's very loud. Listen. Listen. Listen. You will hear why you have made the choices you have made. You will see the pictures of the past that have shaped your current life and may shape your future. It's a cycle. You can change or stop that cycle at any time by realizing the truth (what you have been thinking) and give yourself a new choice. Put in a new thought, one that empowers you (which means that it feels good in your body), choose to believe it, over and over, just like the ego's words that you have been listening to over and over. It has been proven that it takes 21 days to change a habit. This figure is changing daily as We, the collective, progress. The mind ego is habitual. It plays like a tape recording of thoughts from the past over and over. Once you learn what has been running your life unconsciously and you make changes that empower you, your life will change. As you know, the only constant in the universe is change.

This practice served me well as each paradigm I wanted to shift showed up in my life as "just another of those (yucky) experiences I have to deal with." Many people wanted me to share my story and some times they would give me their impressions that were not for me, but for them. I learned two things using this discernment technique:

I always check into my body when people give me information about myself, i.e. an intuitive reader or friend or even a doctor who was trying to help me at

Technique #1: Discernment Technique

my request. If what they said did not check out within my body, a red-flag you might say, I blessed them for the information and let it go. Or, I would ask them some questions to understand better what they were saying, again without taking it on, until I felt right inside myself and then continued the conversation. In the past, I tended to give my power away completely to what others said about me or for me, positive or negative. Since I had no true beliefs about myself, I only had thoughts and feelings that others wanted me to have and I accepted those. Over time this technique helped me to discern the difference between other people's energies and mine, and helped me to tell the truth about my own true feelings.

Often well meaning and kind people will say things to me because it is a message they need to hear. When I feel inside my body and get that constricted feeling, I know the message is not meant for me, but them. I began training myself as a mirror for them in my energy fields, when I felt their thoughts or opinions come to me, I gently close off my chakras (spin them energetically in a counter clockwise position) and listen compassionately to them. As I listen without absorbing, I become their reflection so that their energy goes directly back to them. They become served by their own words and Great Spirit. This practice has become something I teach to most of my clients. It is so empowering to keep your own energy and allow others to be who they are without fixing them or changing their beliefs.

Many have asked about taking on other people's energy. I even hear people say with an air of pride that they are "empathic." In my experience, being empathic is an agreement to feel others feelings. While helpful to some, to others it becomes a burden. Using discernment will allow you to keep your own energy and not "take on others energy." Become masterful about your own energy.

Technique #2

Asking Yourself Empowering Questions

You have the opportunity to expand your consciousness in every moment of every day. You do not need to have a trauma like mine to wake up. You can take your peak experiences, those moments when you get a glimpse of who you are, and expand them.

Begin to restructure your personal priorities so that in every moment of every day you can "know thyself," by asking yourself empowering questions such as: "Is this for my highest good?" "Does this serve me?" "Is this best for me, right now?" "Would I really like this right now?" "Would this feel good to me to do, right now?"

Whenever you are talking to your body make sure you are using a gentle and curious tone. Most people's internal voice is demanding, critical and sarcastic. Sarcasm is the lowest form of communication. Rather, talk to yourself as you choose to be spoken to by others. Before you go to sleep at night review your day, i.e. conversations you had with others, things you completed or did not complete, or plans for the next day. Gently feel into your body for energies that are inharmonious from these conversations. As you connect with these energies, you can add your love to them by asking them in a gentle way "What would you like me to do for you right now?" or "What (about that situation) could have gone better or different?" "What would have felt better?" or "How may I serve you, right now?" By doing this you are clearing your energy before you go to sleep, and setting up your tomorrow to be more effective and powerful for you.

During the night, energies will shift. Your consciousness will be at work shifting and changing you and your cells. When you wake up in the morning you will feel clearer and begin your day more refreshed. If you happen to wake up with less than comfortable energies activated, having you go inside your body, feel those energies and ask the questions above again. Once aware, you can create your day, what you want and then synchronicities will show up for you. On a cellular level you are clear of old energies and patterns that have bothered you in the past. Doing this exercise each night before sleeping will change you in a natural, gentle way, and help you sleep more soundly.

Remember in my introduction I mentioned that commitment to your path is not easy and is without instant gratification?

At first many people tell me they love these exercises and have great results, but when I check back with them about whether they have continued to use them they say they "forgot" or didn't keep up. Answering this response I ask, "What would happen to your life if you kept it up until it became natural for you, a way of keeping your own promises to yourself?" This gentle reminder ignites their own happy results and they can clearly see the difference in their commitment to their path and their daily life choices.

Over time you will find that when something comes your way that isn't for you, you know it instinctively and

Technique #2: Asking Yourself Empowering Questions

you can politely say, "No thank you." Also, your body will begin to relax and you will feel more centered and whole, allowing you to breathe deeply more often. Using this practice for over eight years now, I have found that I have healed and grown spiritually, in a natural way and my life has changed for the better.

Using this technique, I was able to see the times I resisted changes in my life that would have hindered my spiritual growth.

I learned to be very gentle and patient, as well as nonjudgmental of myself. The growth path, or spiritual path does not always look exactly the way you think. Sometimes it comes in ways you might not like, and other times it will appear in more magnificent ways than you could have ever thought possible. However it comes, be gentle with yourself and always be ready to learn how much you are loved. Even some choices I thought were very good ones had to change, because I had healed a choice I made years ago that did not fit any longer. I am constantly upgrading my self, my thinking, and my choices.

Technique #3

Conscious Breathing

You may leave your eyes open or close them, whichever helps you feel empowered, and loosen any clothing that may restrict you in any way. Allow your breath to enter your body through your crown chakra, the top of your head. See and feel this breath as though it is coming into your body through a cylinder that is about the size of your fist. This cylinder is soft and expansive. It holds your prana, your life force.

As you breathe into your crown, accept the love from the entire universe. Allow your breath to flow as you inhale, down your body through the soles of your feet, asking anything that is ready to leave to go with your breath as you exhale. Make portals on the soles of your feet so the breath can leave easily. As you exhale, let go of anything that has come up in your body that is uncomfortable or painful - a hurt, an emotion, a thought, a picture, a sensation of any kind that would take you out of your inner peace. Have the intent that all the energy you have exhaled be transmuted into the highest golden light, to be given to the universe as your gift of letting go. This light mixes with "all love of the universe" and will be utilized anytime others are requesting universal pure love energy. Your life force is a constant gift to you, from the universe as you breathe in. As you release any feelings that do not feel like love to the universe, you are contributing to the welfare of

Technique #3: Conscious Breathing

all beings that are choosing light and love as their path. You see the cycle. You feel the cycle within you. This is your experience of living safely inside your body.

Begin expanding the breath within you. Imagine that the breath has a life of its own and moves within you to every place, even the darkest places. On the next inhale of breath, fill your belly, then your lungs, first lower then upper lungs, then heart, throat, and brain with as much air as you can possibly breathe in. Let it go, gently. Without a pause on the next inhalation do the same process and notice what feelings and thoughts keep coming up, then let them go. As your breath expands within, notice all the new feelings you have not felt before and exhale them, remembering that as they are released they are transmuted into fine light and love to be used by the universe at a later time. With your next breath in add the golden light.

Keep the breathing going and notice how far your breath is willing to be expanded within you. Are there edges to the breath? Notice and feel. On the next breath in, go a bit beyond the edges. Then on the next breath in, go even farther. Eventually, the edges will melt and there will be no difference between you and the air. Rest in this feeling of timelessness and effortlessness.

Call in your Angels, healers, and masters from the other realms. Place yourself within a golden bubble that will protect you as you breathe. This golden bubble is a few inches from your body and will keep this fine golden energy, within you and around you, in place all day and through the night.

Imagine your body as a golden pyramid of light. This golden pyramid keeps fresh and alive the vitality, beauty, energy, youth, health, and characteristics you have always asked for in your body and in your life. As you breathe this breath, feel your life force. You are filled with light filtering in, through and around, your entire body. Keep this breathing going for at least 5 minutes, more if you have the time. If your eyes have closed, then gently open them continuing the breath. Keep this breathing going all day long during all your activities. Notice how energetic and present you feel. Your energy will feel balanced all day, and if you feel a constriction, breathing deeper. Drink some water.

Technique #4

Chakra Toning and Clearing

Your personal sound helps your body heal. When you intentionally make a sound into each of your chakras, you will help your body balance itself, each and every day. And when you add the color of each chakra with the sound or tone and your breath, your personal power is increased for that day.

Begin breathing in through your "prana" cylinder. This time we will make a circular motion through the body, breathing in down the front of the body to meet each chakra, and then up the spine meeting all the charkas again, out the crown, then, the next breath in. Your eyes may naturally close, or you can keep them open, the choice is yours.

Breathe down into your base chakra with the color red and tone a sound that feels right for that chakra. When you make the sound, take your time to find just the right sound for you, the one that is perfect for each area and the one that may even vibrate that chakra. This is not singing to yourself, this is toning a sound that is the natural sound for each chakra in your body. Once you find the right tone for each chakra you will feel the vibration and it will naturally begin to feel good in that area of your body. As you exhale, take that color and sound all the way up your spine. Do this three times.

Next, breathe in to your base and bring the color red into the second chakra then add the color orange and a tone for that energy center, and as you exhale take the red and orange together, toning up the spine. Do this three times.

Next, breathe into your base, second, and third chakras, bringing the red, orange, and now yellow (for the third chakra, or your solar plexus) together with a tone you feel good about. As you exhale, take the colors along with the tone up the spine. Do this three times.

Next, breathe into your base, second, third, and fourth chakras, bringing the colors red, orange, yellow, and green and a sound for the heart center together, and when you exhale take all the colors along with the tone up the spine. Do this three times.

Next, breathe into your base, second, third, fourth, and fifth chakras, bringing the red, orange, yellow, green, and now adding blue to the throat area while toning the perfect sound for that energy center, and when you exhale take all the colors and sound up the spine. Do this three times.

Next, breathe into your base, second, third, fourth, fifth, and sixth chakras, bringing the colors red, orange, yellow, green, blue, and indigo to the point between your eyebrows and tone the sound for that energy center, and when you exhale take all the colors and sound up the spine. Do this three times.

Next, breathe into your base, second, third, fourth, fifth, sixth, and seventh (your crown) chakras, and breathe in red, orange, yellow, green, blue, indigo, and

Technique #4: Chaakra Toning and Clearing

add white (and/or gold) to the crown chakra and the perfect tone for that energy center, and when you exhale take the tone and breath out the top of your head. Do this three times.

One last time, bring your breath into each of the chakras and colors, touching each one with the perfect sound that will resonate with each center and exhale all the breath, sound and colors, creating a rainbow within your body. Now, sit still and feel your body—it's lightness, movement, shifting—and give gratitude to yourself and your body for this moment of pure peace.

Technique #5

Self-Healing Meditation

This is the honored process I learned and ultimately used to heal my body. Even now, when anything comes up in my body, I go to this meditation first to heal. I suggest you tape this in your own voice once you have read it and learn the process. Then if you become ill, or have some emotional energy nagging at you, you can lie down and play it for yourself and walk through the process of self-healing gracefully. When you keep this practice going on a regular basis you will find that you can use it with any situation you are in that is uncomfortable. Since you are so familiar with your body, you can take a few breaths in, focus on what your body needs, and shift your energy quickly by using this technique.

Go deeply inside your body breathing into your prana cylinder. Turn your eyes inward as if you could see your brain, (pause) notice the lights at the end of your eyes showing the way to what you are about to discover. (pause) Notice your Angel there waiting for you, (pause) the one you can count on to teach you, keep you safe, hold your hand along the way, guide you, and remind you that you are loved. Take your angels hand and allow him/her to guide you to a place in your body that is asking for your attention.

Talk to your body as you are taking your consciousness inward toward the pain. Talk to it as if it

Technique #5: Self-Healing Meditation

is your only child. Tell your body how much you have missed being in connection with it all these years—that you know now how much you have neglected and abused it and that you also know how magnificent it is, that it only wants to be healthy, vital, and alive. Let your body know that you are willing to be its partner now. Make a connection so strong that it will know from this moment on that you are going to do whatever you can to make sure your body has everything it needs. Use words that work for you as you continue to talk to your body to create a conscious relationship with it.

Apologize for not always taking care of it and unconsciously allowing it to be left to its own resources and (pause) have gratitude that it has done the best it can without you. Now you are here, in full connection, conscious in the moment, to help it live fully, healthy with grace and ease. (pause) Ask your body to forgive you, and then forgive yourself, and feel what it feels like to be forgiven for all the years of neglect.

Visit the painful area(s) (Pain is an acronym for, Pay Attention Inside Now) See it exactly as it is—on all sides. Notice what shape it is, size it is, color, and if it has a sound or texture. See it as clearly as you can, in detail. (pause)

Next, from your consciousness, keep your mind in a curious manner without any knowing from the past, just curiosity. Use your breath and consciousness to direct it to the part of your body that is in pain allowing the cells in your body to give you the answer you are here to discover, while you ask for the message this body part would like to communicate to you now. "What am I learning from this pain?" Or "What are you wanting me to know right now?" Or "How may I help you right now?" (pause)

Use all your senses, especially the ones easiest to access, such as seeing, hearing and feeling. Listen with respect and true compassion, to the denial you have lived with, surfacing at your request, and honor the hidden truths ready to be revealed to you. Or, watch the vision, and know you are responsible for what happened as much as being victimized by it.

Or, feel the truth of the pain and know its origination point as it is felt inside you. Forgive every person, including yourself, and every situation including yourself. This has only been the Divine plan, played out for you in a story so you would remember that all you are is love, and that you have waited until now to learn (to remember) the truth is perfect. Thank every person, and situation for playing its part perfectly in your Divine plan, if remembering who you are. Remember you are connected to your Spirit guides and Angels, so you are safe in this re-experience of events.

Notice how your body feels before moving on to the next step. If better, go to the next step. If worse, take a breath and go deeper through the energy of the last answer you got and ask the question again, knowing that there is another cell waiting to reveal some information to you. Or, ask what else you can glean from this pain, or how you got to this point, and continue observing. (pause)

This is a good time to create a dialog with your body. Keep your questions clear and unattached, like "What

Technique #5: Self-Healing Meditation

else would you like me to know right now?" Let the mind watch, and only ask inventive questions like, "Tell me more." "What am I learning from this?" Stay away from asking "Why." When you feel some relief and know the story is complete, go to the next step.

Flood this part of the body with a brilliant, luminescent, sparkling, white light. Connect to your field of pure potential (that place where your Spirit guides and higher self exist), the grid that connects your human body to the entire Universe. The light inside you, as you breathe it in, is the connection and where healing occurs. Allow the color of light to be whatever your body wants, needs, and asks for. (pause)

Allow the light to change colors to support your healing.

See, feel, or hear this part of your body move into its highest perfected form. (If you are not sure how that part of your body looks when it is completely healthy, you can use an anatomy book to find out.) (pause) See all the molecules, atoms, cells, muscles, bones, tissue layers, blood, white cells, red cells, and the part of your body that needed attention, move into its perfected state, as if brand new. Watch it! It is so beautiful to watch your body heal before your very eyes, with ease and freedom. Mix the light into what you are seeing.

Allow the light and your connection to expand within your body. Watch every cell form into healthy perfect cell(s) to be used by the rest of this area and build perfect bones, muscles, organs, tissues, skin or whatever you are working on. Fill every dark place. Every part that wants to hide, let go and surrender to the light.

(pause) While your body is filling with this beautiful white or colored light, forgive yourself for not knowing how to properly take care of your body before, and anything else you would like to forgive from yourself. Feel what it feels like to be in total forgiveness.

Take a few moments and rest in that feeling of forgiveness. (pause)

[Note: This part of the process can seem like a death experience, and once accustomed to the intensity of this light and the feeling of completely letting go to your body's inner wisdom, you will no longer be afraid of death. In fact, you will no longer be afraid of life—of living. Your confidence and self-love will be paramount in your life. Your assertion abilities will be gentler with yourself as with others in your life. You will speak your truth with compassion, for now you understand that there is truly no one else out there; for you are truly everyone and everyone is, YOU! Any kindness or harshness you give to others is also given to yourself. Do you remember that childhood saying, "I'm rubber you are glue, whatever you say to me bounces off and sticks to you?" I have learned that this is very true. When I actually embraced the fact, that I am One with every other being, I began noticing that my thoughts of revenge, blame and retaliation really did hurt ME! This realization sent me on a search to find another way to communicate clearly, and gently, to people, whether they were close relatives, friends or just acquaintances. It does not matter. They are all me,

Technique #5: Self-Healing Meditation

and I am choosing to treat myself with love, therefore, that is how I in turn treat them.]

Gently thank your body for its ability to heal before your very eyes as you thank your Angels and bring your eyes back into their sockets, and gently open them. (pause)

Feel your body, its energy, and allow your consciousness to rest in what just happened. The you that you have known is beautifully transforming, transmuting into a higher vibration of energy. Watch how you feel when you wake the next morning—your dreams, your grace as you go through your day. Sleep, rest—as your body communicates to you its request for sleep. Eat as your body guides you—it is enlivening. Support it! It is cleansing, detoxifying—listen to its cravings, even when they do not seem to make sense to you. Your mind cannot know what is best for your body until your body retrains your mind to listen. Your body will NEVER lie to you. You can trust that!

In this process you will meet your Self face to face. A face you will never forget. Your soul's face . . . and you will never give up on your Self again.

Pay Attention Inside Now!

As of the printing of this book, I have been asked to teach the self-healing practice to people who are already living a life of service and who would like to use this modality to assist their clients or themselves to deeper healing. If you are interested in having a class in your area to learn The Jai Approach or attending one near you, contact me at the information at the front of this book. My website always has current information.

The Law of Life

Whatever you give away today or think or say or do will multiply about tenfold and then return to you.

It may not come immediately nor from the obvious source, but the LAW applies unfailingly through some invisible force.

Whatever you feel about another, be it love or hate or passion, will surely bounce right back to you in some clear or secret fashion.

If you speak about some person, a word of praise or two, soon tons of other people will speak kind words to you.

Our thoughts are broadcasts of the soul, not secrets of the brain. Kind ones bring us happiness, petty ones, untold pain.

Giving works as surely as reflections in a mirror. If hate you send, hate you'll get back, but loving brings love nearer.

Remember, as you start this day, and duty crowds your mind, that kindness comes so quickly back, to those who first are kind!

Let that thought and this one direct you through each day.... The only things we ever keep are the things we give away!

"The miracle is not to walk on water. The miracle is to walk on the green earth in the present moment, to appreciate

the peace and beauty that are available now.... It is not a matter of faith; it is a matter of practice."

Author Unknown

~~NOTES~~

Postscript

The story you have just read is true. The quest that ensued following my fall has seen many ups and downs, disowning prior beliefs, noticing the formulas I had set up as structures and then learning to unlearn them. The energy that I was privileged to live in during that four weeks of healing is not solid—it breathes, expands, and gives life to an enormous amount of love. Can this be sustained? I have wanted to believe and teach that the answer is "Yes," and it is not. What can be sustained is knowing who you truly are: a never ending unearthing of the true self, as a reenactment of prior life choices playing out in this paradigm, blueprint, and moment in time.

We are living in the beginning of a new Millennium. We can brave and even champion our own demons by embracing their inability to appear as love. We can honor that we have minds that play out structures for us to see who we truly are through others. Please do not believe it is forever, or that the answer you have received for yourself one day is THE permanent answer for you. It is not. Your mind will want to know, and maybe for a time that will be appropriate, but that knowing cannot be the Truth. That truth is ever evolving, breathing with who you are, where your consciousness is, from moment to moment.

Your mind will eventually become your support system. Yes, as you move from old patterns, beliefs, and programming and begin to offer yourself new loving ways to talk to yourself, within three weeks—possibly sooner—you will begin to hear these new

Postscript

thoughts coming up instead of the past programming. We are process oriented and our minds are tape recorders. Now that you are putting in new information, the mind's tape recording begins a new track, then when a similar situation comes up, the mind will tell you the new healed version rather than the old conditioning. We are evolving within our own minds!

Also, you are transmuting energies all day long. Your body is also transmuting energies all day long. Our bodies are adapting to what is needed on this earth right now. We came here to have victory over our circumstances, the times we are living in and to learn about transformation. We are going to it anyway, we might as well be conscious about it. I will not give up on myself, no matter what! If I can win, so can you!

When my clients want to know how and why certain structures work the way they do, I tell them there is an explanation and a practice that can support their life changes. Just by virtue of my sharing this with them, the programming is activated. The possibility that my own mind will follow that structure and look for validation in my own life is available. The mind now has my full attention, and its power will play out and create many scenarios and new habits in my life. When this happens then I'm caught in my mind, believing the structures/constructs of it and not who I truly am. From here, life is tenuous. Until we choose. Catching these programmed thoughts and breaking the cycle of them is how you will stay in the moment and free yourself.

Please know this—we are all "One" sharing experiences. Since my healing in 1997, I have been truly happy, and see myself riding a wave of focus that gives my heart great joy and purpose. Even in times when events of life would seem to be unhappy or distressing—they are just that—it doesn't mean anything else. There is no story attached to what's happening. When you are present things just happen, life happens, it does not have to take you away from your internal peace, joy, and happiness, which are your true states of being. When you take care of these life events without your internal peace disappearing and the mind of the past taking over, then you are living in the present moment. That is it! That is all we are to do here. We are all equals in this journey, and it is crucial to put no one's head above yours, or your head above another's.

The respect and grace you have or do not have in your life is directly related to knowing your true Self and your purpose. This is directly tied to your respect for your process, your grace that you are doing the best you can in your life, and your state of peace, which creates an existence filled with as much love as you can possibly let in.

Truth be told, my life is not always as together as some people would like to think and as I (ego) like to sometimes project out. Sometimes it is tough, hard, difficult, and unhappy. AND, in each situation whatever is happening, I am the best that I can be at that time fully allowing and accepting my humanness and feeling state. Sometimes I am in my own

Postscript

constructs of mind and its consciousness doing the best I can with the knowledge I have at the time, choosing to honor both my small self and my true Self. When my consciousness is in a "funky" or negative place, I allow it as long as it takes for me to get to my truth at which time it shifts and a choice is revealed or consciously made.

This is and is not magic. It is, because accepting the negative constructs by experiencing them brings grace and spontaneity which allows you to see and feel the magic. It is not, because it was there all along. You just didn't have your perspective in the truth so it looked other than magic. It truly is that simple. Our perceptions are all we have. When we are aware of our perceptions we can choose to honor our personal truth and the truth we are choosing to live into.

God is always there in every moment, so there is no waiting. Just let your perceptions go with God.

God bless you!

Sheryl Jai,
A celebrated re-birth into gratitude 4/26/1997

Appendix

The New Teacher

I feel the following information is key for people to know about the spiritual times we are living in right now, the way energies are changing, and how you may expect your spiritual teachers are changing as well.

This appendix was written by my friend. She is an international teacher, author, mystic, and guide presently living in Sedona, Arizona. We have both learned to respect the growth and value of the teachings coming to us right now in so many new forms. If you would like to contact her personally, her information is listed at the end of this section. In respect for Aluna, this appendix is unedited.

The New Teacher
by Aluna Joy Yaxk'in

You are not going to like the new teacher. The new teacher will ask you questions instead of giving you the answers. The new teacher won't tell you how to think, or tell you which path you should be on. And, the new teacher won't tell you what to do. The new teacher will tell stories instead of preach, and let you arrive at the answer that is right for you.

The New Teacher

The new teacher will not make your choices for you, and is not here to carry your weight on the path. The new teacher will inspire you to gain strength and confidence, so you can walk that path on your own. The new teacher wants you to be independent, not dependent. The new teacher wants to walk with you . . . not have you follow behind.

The new teacher will not limit your possibilities for the new teacher knows that there are a multitude of paths all going to the same destination. For this reason, the new teacher will never say, "My way is the only way." The new teacher wants you to awaken to the God power you have inside. The new teacher will never offer students a spiritual shortcut. The new teacher is a hard core realist. The new teacher knows that spiritual progress usually comes step-by-step over time and with dedication, but is also open to the magical fact that spontaneous awakenings do happen.

The new teacher will never make negative prophecies, because of the understanding that the position of teacher can influence many people. If the new teacher influences others into a state of fear, this knowing may become blocked from the students' ability to access truth from Spirit themselves. The new teacher also has power over the collective consciousness. The new teacher knows that by putting out negative predictions, it might influence the entire collective fabric and create limitations; thus making our work at this time unnecessarily harder. The new teacher knows fear stops you from hearing your own inner truth.

The new teacher won't be impressed by gifts or compliments, as many teachers don't want to be teachers at all. You might find the new teacher in the most unusual places. A teacher might be a downtrodden character sitting next to you in a little café, or you might find the new teacher in a place you might likely expect. The new teacher will be everywhere, and could be anyone. God works through all people in countless ways.

The new teacher will not try to win you over by promising you spiritual phenomena (a form of metaphysical entertainment) or with grandiose visions. It might be fun, but it doesn't get you very far on the path. Spiritual phenomena may or may not show up around your spiritual teacher, or you. However, if it does enter your path, enjoy the journey. If it doesn't show up, enjoy the journey anyway!

The new teacher is not status oriented. Status, or the use of titles, may mean to some that one person is better than another and creates separation. Status or title empowers one, while disempowering another, and this is not acceptable. The new teacher will not be impressed by who you were in the past, the experiences you have had, or how much you know unless they are relevant to the present. The new teacher will not be much impressed with your degrees, titles, and exalted positions. The new teacher does not care about your genetic heritage, how much education you have had, or who you have worked with. All they care about is who you are right now. The new teacher will be real with you, and hopes that you will be real back. After all, who we were in the past is just that . . . the past. That was then, this is now. All the new teacher cares about is where your heart is now, because nothing else matters but NOW.

Aluna Joy Yaxk'in, Author, Mystic and Guide.
CENTER of the SUN
PO Box 1988
Sedona, AZ 86339 USA
PH: 928-282-6929
Webpage: http://www.alunajoy.com/
Email: alunajoy@kachina.net

~~NOTES~~

Acknowledgements

If you have only one prayer, let be of gratitude

I choose to acknowledge every person I have had the grace to become acquainted with in this life. Each one has taught me powerfully through their wisdom. Even though they may not know it, I learned from each of them. Through the feelings in my body and mind - I have and am learning the lessons I am here to embody and evolve my soul. You know who you are. Thank You.

Teachers come in many forms, physical and non-physical. I am clear that the majority of my healing has been assisted by non-physical beings. I wish to acknowledge with deep gratitude God, the Angels, the Archangels, the Earth, the Sky, the four directions and elementals, the dimensions, the animals - all of nature's creation.

With each name listed here, in no particular order, know that I appreciate and love each one of you with all my heart.   My deepest thanks to:

My children, Kimberly and Tod Kubo, who came to my aid and were willing to stay as long as needed. That meant more to me than you will ever know. I love you.

Dee Dee Shalinda, spiritual counseling, past life regressions, and always being there with an open heart and loving ears; Andras Nevai, axiotonal gridwork, and the best hugs; Sheila Denny, the gift of loving hands and multiple talents; Ryah, Neuro-link and generous financial support at the beginning of my travels to teach; Diane Goulder-Steineger, for emotional and generous financial support at the beginning of my teaching; Diane Warren, Reiki and angelic love; Marianna Hartsong, Trager and seasoned wisdom; Anne Lemieux, Body Wisdom Lomi Lomi, delightful hands and heart; Cynthia Chu, multi-dimensional bodywork with ancient wisdom; Marylou Brown, lymphatic massage and angelic messages of love; Candace McGinnis, healer and angelic energy worker and messenger; Stan Sneag, for his dedication and love; Anita Tamboli, for always being there with a smile and loving heart; Lew and Francine Epstein for teaching me to trust that I am loved; Vonn Harting, for teaching me Conscious Language and how to heal using essential oils; Gary Young, master alchemist for essential oils; Bob & Helena Stevens, The Mastery of Language; Henry Herzberger, my scholarly Vedic teacher; Dr. David Milgrim, Chiropractor, Medicine man and multi-dimensional gridwork; Dr. Timothy Bonatus, Orthopaedic Surgeon with friendly smiles, open attitude and support for this book; Dr. Lee, Anesthesiologist, thanks for the surprise ending; the entire staff of Flagstaff Medical, nurses, aides, pre and post op and the physical therapist; Karon Miller and Bob Yettner without whom I would have done that hike; and to my best friend, Trisha Blanden for continuing love, encouragement, and support.

Thanks to my brilliant book mentors for teaching me about writing and believing in me. Eve Hogan, Kate Ramsey, Peggy Philips, Nancy Grace (my muse), Virginia Joy Smith, Roger Jellinek, and so many

Acknowledgements

editors, Patricia Haller, Jannah Reimer, Anita Tamboli, Talia Miller, Char Thomas. My awesome layout assistant Erin Gilpin, and to Larry Morningstar for all you do and are. I am deeply moved by each of your commitments to this project.

Recommended Reading

These are some of my favorite authors. I am most inspired by them. They are all great teachers, so when you choose a book to read, choose from your heart and the reading will empower you.

Louise Hay, "You Can Heal Your Life"
Tom Kenyon and Virginia Essene, "The Hathor Material"
Marianne Williamson, "The Healing of America"
Deepak Chopra, "Perfect Health"
David R. Hawkins, "Power vs. Force"
Michael Talbot, "The Holographic Universe"
Paramahansa Yogananda, "Autobiography of a Yogi"
The Course In Miracles
Eugene E. Whitworth, "Nine Faces of Christ"
Neale Donald Walsch, "Conversations with God" series
J.J. Hurtak, "The Keys of Enoch"
"The Course in Miracles"

Of course, there are many, many more . . . reading is a great opportunity to expand our perceptions. Enjoy! The most appropriate book for you, at the most appropriate time, will come to you, keep your eyes open.

Glossary

Angels – Ethereal beings that live in the dimensions of the Universe. Known by many names, the angels ascend some each time you ask for them to help you. They are a gift to us at this time, while the earth and our collective consciousness is going through its changes. We can ask them specifically to assist our life's challenges by simply stating: Health (or specific problem) Angel, please help me with (<u>example: this headache</u>)", Car Angel, please help me with ____", Money Angel, thank you for helping me with ___." Be as specific as you are aware. We can have anything we want, when we learn to ask. You have many angels around you, begin a practice every moment of the day taking your awareness off of you and asking the angels to help you with whatever you are experiencing.

Be With – an expression used to identify a way of being with something, as to "be with" the discomfort of pain, it is to melt into the pain, allow it, surrender to it, not be distracted by anything else, giving what you are "being with" your full attention and presence.

Blueprint – the dictionary definition is: a design, plan or other technical drawing. Spiritually we are responsible to this plan. I believe that we designed the plan of our life's existence on this earth plane at this time before we came here in a body. The way we live our lives, all of the circumstances, the people and all the events are part of that designed plan as part of our conscious evolution.

Chakras – edited with permission from the website http://www.sacredcenters.com/chakras.html. The word chakra is Sanskrit for wheel or disk and signifies one of seven basic energy centers in the body. Each of these centers correlates to major nerve ganglia branching forth from the spinal column. In addition the chakras also correlate to levels of consciousness, archetypal elements, developmental stages of life, colors, sounds, and body functions to list a few.

Chakra Seven – *Thought, Universal identity, oriented to self-knowledge.*
This is the crown chakra that relates to consciousness as pure awareness. It is our connection to the greater world beyond, to a timeless, spaceless place of all-knowing. When developed, this chakra brings us knowledge, wisdom, understanding, spiritual connection, and bliss.

Chakra Six – *Light, Archetypal identity, oriented to self-reflection.*
This chakra is known as the brow chakra or third eye center. It is related to the act of seeing, both physically and intuitively. As such it opens our psychic faculties and our understanding of archetypal levels. When healthy it allows us to see clearly, in effect, letting us "see the big picture."

Glossary

Chakra Five – *Sound, Creative identity, oriented to self-expression.*
This is the chakra located in the throat and is thus related to communication. Here we experience the world symbolically through vibration, such as the vibration of sound representing language.

Chakra Four – *Air, Social identity, oriented to self-acceptance.*
This chakra is called the heart chakra and is the middle chakra in a system of seven. It is related to love and is the integrator of opposites in the psyche: mind and body, male and female, persona and shadow, ego and unity. A healthy fourth chakra allows us to love deeply, feel compassion, have a deep sense of peace and centeredness.

Chakra Three – *Fire, Ego identity, oriented to self-definition*
This chakra is known as the power chakra, located in the solar plexus. It rules our personal power, will, and autonomy, as well as our metabolism. When healthy, this chakra brings us energy, effectiveness, spontaneity, and non-dominating power. It is the place where you feel your gut intuition as well as when someone is taking power from you or you are giving them your power. It is where you use your will either positively or negatively.

Chakra Two – *Water, Emotional identity, oriented to self-gratification*

The second chakra, located in the abdomen, lower back, and sexual organs, is related to the element water, and to emotions, creativity, reproduction and sexuality. It connects us to others through feeling, desire, sensation, and movement. Ideally this chakra brings us fluidity and grace, depth of feeling, sexual fulfillment, creating our lives through goals, vision and dreams and the ability to accept change.

Chakra One –*Earth, Physical identity, oriented to self-preservation, tribal, belonging.*
Located at the base of the spine, this chakra forms our foundation. It represents the element earth, and is therefore related to our survival instincts, and to our sense of grounding and connection to our bodies and the physical plane. Ideally this chakra brings us health, prosperity, security, and dynamic presence. It can also be the reason we act out of fear and deep seeded past based beliefs.

Choice – One of the biggest "aha's" in my life was to understand true choice. Choice is one of the most liberating words in our language. Once you have considered all aspects of something, gone through all the ideas and thoughts about that something and completely understand your own reasoning, you can choose based on nothing, just because you can. It is without consideration or reasoning. Coming from a place of freedom within, not what you think you should do, or what others think you should do, or what you

Glossary

have always done, or what you think others think you should do, but choosing because you can choose.

Clearing Energies – I will share some of the powerful techniques that I use. These days, more people are asking me "How do I keep my energy clear?" and "How do I release energies I feel that are not mine?" One of my teachers Helene Rothschild taught me to **clear energies** around me or entities that get stuck on me, as my frequency raises, by calling in Archangel Michael and his sword of light to swish the energies to the light and say "Will you help me let go of these energies and take them to go to the light, to Source." I also like to ask Saint Germaine and his violet flame to come and circle the violet flame around my body from top to bottom as I say the same prayer. Another way is to **close off your chakras** every morning before you leave your house for the day, visualize your chakras turning counter clockwise until closed, you will feel it. One of my favorite techniques is to surround myself with a **golden bubble**. Gold is one of the strongest and most precious metals used for healing and synonymous with Christ's love. This golden bubble will protect you from outside energies and entities and keep the love within you growing. Visualize your energy fields filled with golden light and claim that you are surrounded with golden light, that nothing can penetrate the golden shield around you and that your personal energy remains connected to source.

Discern – I am asking people to use discernment as a skill. To be able to notice how things are, feel into your own body to test if it is good for you and learn to trust and follow your own body's advice. You can learn to discern on your own by allowing the mind to go on vacation while you ask the body for its inner wisdom. When you let go of the mind, the body's inner wisdom will give you the correct answer, and you know it's correct because it feels right.

Grace – Of five definitions, the closest definition that Oxford American dictionary uses to my meaning is: a divinely given talent or blessing. For me, grace is an energy. Grace has come to me many times as I have grown and healed. Sometimes grace stays around for a few days, sometimes I don't feel it for a while. Grace feels to me like a gift given from the heavens when my experience of life is lived in the moment.

Guidance – Hearing words inside your mind which you did not generate. The energy of the voice is stronger (this can be soft or loud) and more powerful than you know your own mind's voice's energies to be. By asking it questions you can learn about yourself, your life and be directed or guided in your everyday thoughts and actions. It is very important right now, to learn to discern this voice from your ego voice. First of all, you can discern by asking the empowering question, "Are you of the light?" If the guidance is not of the light it will have to disappear. You can trust this – the light will never lie or come from fear or put you in fear, in

Glossary

any way. As soon as you ask the question, if information or the voice is not of the light, it will dissipate. Ask if this is for your highest good to know right now or to be in action about. This way you will not be taking on things or doing things that are ego directions. I learned to discern the difference between my thought/ego thoughts, which are based in the past and are very familiar versus the voices that are giving me directions. I follow that direction without hesitation; directions which I would have never thought of before. Your life will change as you trust this voice and let go of your ego.

The Order of Melchizedek – The Order of Melchizedek is from the ancient mystery school teachings during the time of Jesus. The order emanates the teachings of love, harmony, and living "right" will or God's will. The teachings and energy of Melchizedek radiate love. If you resonate with this energy or the word Melchizedek and would like to have more information or be ordained, there is only one person on this earth who has been given the right to do these ordinations, his name is Dan Chesbro. Contact him at (585) 346-9667 or sanbeloved@aol.com for his schedule.

Mirror – When we are living in a state of Oneness, we experience others as ourselves. As we grow and heal we can look to those around us as mirror reflections. As we listen to what is said to us, using the mirror, we can clearly see ourselves. As we share with others our experiences, we are learning what we have shared at a deeper level. This concept says that "no one is out there, it's all you (me)."

Multi-Dimensional Brain – To have a scientific explanation that matches my understanding may take more research than available to me at this time. I will be explaining this in more detail in my next book. For now, I will tell you that your brain accepts many energies that stimulate your existence; that is, messages or imprinting that you receive that you identify as you. This is a simplistic way of understanding a very complex instrument: your beautiful brain. Your brain has the capacity to be open to, like a gateway, energies that are other than of this world. If you choose to allow this opening consciously, you may feel and be present to many different types of stimulus that will empower your life.

Om Namah Shivaya – According to the website www.answers.com Shiva is one of the principal Hindu deities, worshiped as the destroyer and restorer of worlds and in numerous other forms. Om, is the supreme and most sacred symbol and sound in the universe. Namah in Hindu means "I bow to thee."

Oy – A Jewish expression similar to "oh no."

Paradigm – A typical example or pattern of something; a model. As an example, many say that our society lives in a paradigm of consumerism. This

Glossary

paradigm then has its own way of influencing people through TV, the media, newspapers, advertising, even when you are shopping there are stimuli (through the senses) that will make you purchase more without you knowing it. This is one way of explaining paradigms; there are many other explanations and many other paradigms that we live with.

Psychic Abilities – Everyone is psychic, everyday you make choices based on what you get psychically from the world around you. Some people have these gifts tuned up and others are unaware of them. Some people choose to learn to empower their psychic abilities. Whatever your choice these definitions and experiences may assist you.

Clairaudience – Oxford American dictionary states: the supposed faculty of perceiving, as if by hearing, what is inaudible. This sense came during my healing at home. One night I was awakened to a beautiful noise. The whirring inside my head came from absolute silence. Through the depths of silence there is a whirl of energy that has sound within it, as part of it. I call it the Universal Hum. After that night, I began hearing things that weren't being said by people around me. For instance, while grocery shopping as I walked by a person, I heard their inner thoughts. The voice wasn't mine and as I passed by them the voice would fade. I only heard the few thoughts that were in their mind at the moment I walked by them. Once I realized what was happening, and while very grateful for this gift, I asked my angels for it to be turned off and only used when I'm in service to a person. This was done immediately. This ability is also hearing spirit's messages clearly, your own inner guidance.

Clairsentience – this ability is feeling. Once I was healed and began going out of my house again, I realized that I felt everything around me. I felt the trees, the car, the concrete, the sky, the birds, it did not matter whether it was alive or inanimate, I felt every bit of it.

Clairvoyance – Oxford American dictionary states: the supposed faculty of perceiving things or events in the future or beyond normal sensory contact. The moment I woke up and spoke out loud on the mountain I immediately became aware that my inner vision was opened. I saw things I had not seen before. Lights flashing around people, shapes of people that were not physical, energies moving inter-dimensionally around me and others as well as being able to see very clearly within my body, every particle as it was (unhealthy) or (healed). I have done many readings for people on their physical body, medical issues, relationships, and careers. I helped one person locate a missing relative, many with real estate transactions, stock tips and various other questions people would like answers to that do not have their own clairvoyance tuned up. Anyone can do this, if you really want it.

Glossary

Sabotage – When you have a goal or dream going in one direction and a conflict in your body, thoughts or emotions that says you cannot have that. This conflict will thwart your own attempts at creating something new for yourself. The actions you take are unconscious, they are in your subconscious patterning or programming and are so habitual you cannot even see that you are doing things opposing your dream or goal.

Separation – Genesis 3: 10; Isiah 59: 2. Cut off from the Source of Life, death progressively spreads to every area of his existence. (from website http://www.greatcom.org/resources/turning_the_tables/ch_22/default.htm). When we do not "know thyself" we are separated from God, nature, other people and from ourselves. We believe we are alone. This is a mistake and not true. Even though it seems real and we may even have loads of evidence to prove this feeling and belief is true, it is not. When we "know thyself" we experience miracles, we thrive, we know we are never alone, we have peace and serene lives and emanate that energy to others. This will be explained in deeper detail in my next book.

Theta – Meditation, Intuition and memory. Going deeper into relaxation, you enter the elusive and mysterious Theta state where brain activity slows almost to the point of sleep, but not quite. Theta is the brain state where magic happens in the crucible of your own neurological activity. Theta brings forward heightened receptivity, flashes of dreamlike imagery, inspiration, and your long-forgotten memories. Theta can bring you deep states of meditation. A sensation of "floating." And because it is an expansive state, in Theta, you may feel your mind expand beyond the boundaries of your body. Theta rests directly on the threshold of your subconscious. In Biofeedback, it is most commonly associated with the deepest levels of meditation. Theta also plays an important part in behavior modification programs and has been used in the treatment of drug and alcohol addiction. Finally, Theta is an ideal state for super-learning, re-programming your mind, dream recall, and self-hypnosis. Theta waves range between 4-7 HZ. Theta is one of the more elusive and extraordinary realms we can explore. It is also known as the twilight state which we normally only experience fleetingly as we rise up out of the depths of delta upon waking, or drifting off to sleep. In Theta, we are in a waking dream, vivid imagery flashes before the mind's eye and we are receptive to information beyond our normal conscious awareness. Theta has also been identified as the gateway to learning and memory. Theta meditation increases creativity, enhances learning, reduces stress, and awakens intuition and other extrasensory perception skills.

Yom Kippor – The Jewish High Holy Days are observed during the 10-day period between the first day (Rosh Hashanah) and the 10th day (Yom Kippur) of Tishri, the seventh month of the Jewish calendar. Rosh Hashanah and Yom Kippur are the most highly

Glossary

regarded of all Jewish Holidays and the only holidays that are purely religious, as they are not related to any historical or natural event. Rosh Hashanah, the Jewish New Year, is celebrated the first and second days of Tishri. It is a time of family gatherings, special meals, and sweet tasting foods. Yom Kippur, the Day of Atonement, is the most solemn day of the Jewish year and is observed on the tenth day of Tishri. It is a day of fasting, reflection and prayers.

Printed in the United States
200596BV00001B/1-51/A